Taking Charge of Your Child's Education

▲

Nine Steps to Becoming a Learning Ally

Terry Mallen

Illustrated by Joe Myers

Acumen Press   ▲   Seattle, WA

Taking Charge of Your Child's Education:
Nine Steps to Becoming a Learning Ally

Copyright © Terry Mallen 1995

Book design by Janice Wall
Illustrated by Joe Myers

Library of Congress Catalog Card Number: 94-72481
ISBN: 0-9642369-9-0

Attention: Schools and Parent Groups:
This book is available at a quantity discount with bulk purchases for educational use. For information, please write to: ACUMEN Press, P.O. Box 16385, Seattle, WA 98116.

Printed in the United States of America

Table of Contents

To Antigoni

Acknowledgments

I suspect there's a point in time when all books are born. The collection of ideas and notes that might end up as an essay or article are seen in a new light. The author surveys the material on his desk and says with astonishment, "Whoa, I've got a book here!"

I guess that's the way it happens. Of course it didn't happen that way with me. Startling revelations have never been my strong suit. Yes, I had all the material and yes, it was threatening to consume all my office space, but I wasn't aware of its potential. I thought all I had was a mess. It was only in response to my confusion over what to do with the material that my good friend, Jan Wall, said, "Well Terry, it sounds as if you've got a book here."

Thus the first person I'd like to acknowledge is Jan Wall, because she induced the labor that culminated in the birth of this project. Without her prodding I might still be pushing piles of material around my office. Jan is also responsible for the way this book looks. She designed every page as well as the cover, and has given the book the inviting yet efficient look I was seeking.

Migael Scherer edited the book and in the process, taught me what it means to be a writer. Just as importantly, though, Migael demonstrated how an author addresses the world. Through her gentle example I learned that courage and a willingness to risk are often as important as literary skills. Migael possesses all of these attributes. A writer as well as an editor, she "walks the talk" of her advice, and in so doing is the model for much of what I believe about a Learning Ally.

Before my words there were Joe Myers' pictures. I decided I wanted Joe to illustrate the book before the first sentence was written. I had only seen a sample of his work, but was immediately taken by his characters. They were in my mind as I wrote and they came spilling out of Joe's pen when he finally got the manuscript. Joe combined a keen sense of what I wanted with his own wonderfully oblique world-view. To call the match of words and pictures ideal is not an exaggeration.

Mark Jaroslaw deserves thanks as well for his valuable advice on independent publishing. He generously shared his experience as a writer and publisher throughout the final stages of this project. His counsel was encouraging and it saved me from untold amounts of grief.

I'd like to thank Dr. Gene Sharratt and Vera Risdon for taking the time to read the manuscript and Phyllis Hatfield who did a final, scrupulous proofreading of the text.

Finally I'd like to acknowledge the pivotal role my wife, Antigoni, played in this book. It isn't always enough to know you have the experience and skills to succeed. Sometimes you need another person to believe in you. My wife gave me the gift of her faith, and I'm unceasingly grateful.

Introduction

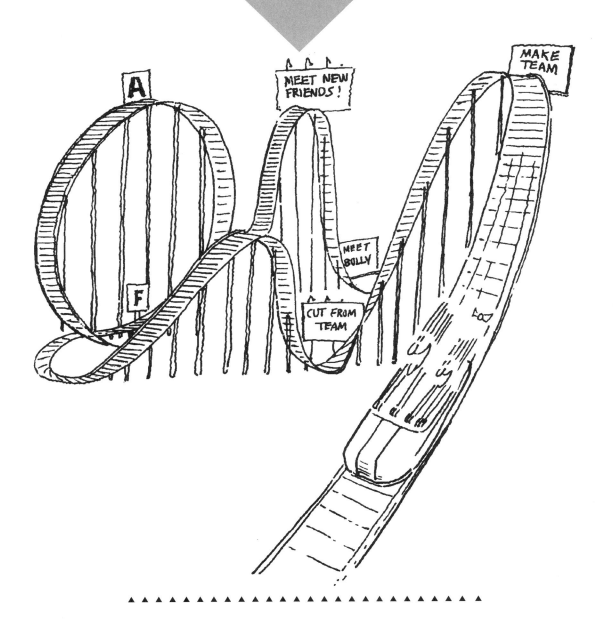

Of all the people involved in
your child's education,
you are the most important.

Teachers, principals,
specialists, librarians,
counselors, custodians:
none have the impact that
you have. Administrators,
curriculum designers,
coaches, bus drivers, crossing
guards: all their influence
pales compared to yours.

This is a book about recognizing that influence and taking action. It doesn't matter what your relationship to the young learner is. You may be a parent or guardian, a grandparent, or simply a person who is committed to a child's personal and academic development. What does matter is acting upon the knowledge that you are the most important person in that student's learning world. You will never be involved in a more worthy, more noble effort!

It doesn't matter if your child is failing. It doesn't matter if he or she is an "underachiever" (whatever that is!) or has been identified as a learner with "problems" or a "gifted student" (whatever those are!). The activities in this book help because they are built upon a conviction that everyone can learn and everyone can improve.

In twelve years of teaching, I never encountered a situation where a kid couldn't be helped. There was never a case where the parent and student sat down with me and we couldn't come up with a program for improvement. Never!

In fact, just the action of talking together often made a world of difference. Taking action leads to solutions. This is a book of solutions that only require your action to make them real.

You may be wondering, "If I'm the most important person in their education, who's gonna do their work? Especially the calculus!"

Don't worry, the kid will still be the kid. They'll still attend the school, do the work and earn the marks. They will be responsible for their efforts and take credit for their achievements. You, on the other hand, will be the person I call the "Learning Ally."

This is a book about the things a Learning Ally does. It's primarily concerned with "what to do" rather than "why." Although I include some of the reasons and rationales for the activities recommended, I only touch lightly on those aspects. It's my belief that most people are less concerned with the philosophy behind a particular approach and more concerned with its effectiveness. My goal is to give you "stuff" that works!

In no way is this a book about inaction. It's not about waiting around for your young person to outgrow their difficulties—they rarely do. It's not about waiting for schools, teachers, and administrators to learn how to meet your needs—they don't have time, or are too busy keeping the whole system afloat. It's not a book about waiting and hoping. It's about doing things today, tomorrow, and in the next weeks that will ensure your child's academic success.

This book will provide you with a roadmap for achievement. It will show you a path through the often confusing jungle of education. You are going to clear and enlarge this path yourself. Using tools that consist of doable, logical actions, you as a parent or supportive adult will become a trusted guide, a Learning Ally. You'll lead your youngster right through the jungle to the other side.

One of the biggest rewards for you will be an improved relationship with your child. The activities I outline will ease you out of the role of punisher and nagger. What may at first have been time you allotted with a bit of a grudge, will soon be transformed into quality time that smacks of recreation more than work.

The more of these activities you incorporate, the more likely you are to have success in helping your student do better work. Who knows? Your youngster might even surpass that level. After all, they now have a Learning Ally!

What Is a Learning Ally?

A Learning Ally is a role quite different from the one you may have played up to this point. It's a role based on the **value** you put on your young person, not on what they achieve. It's a role based on things you **do** for them, not on any qualities you may have as a person.

There's not a kid around who doesn't know the importance of studying hard and earning high marks. Spending time trying to convince them of that is wasted, because they already know it!

What they don't often know is the value you put on them as individuals. I contend that they won't value their schoolwork until they are convinced they are of value themselves. Convincing them of their own unique merit is your job.

Becoming a Learning Ally does just that. It enables you to constantly send the message that your young person counts, that they're worthy. It's a role that frees you from obsessing about *performance* and lets you concentrate on *improvement*. A Learning Ally focuses on possibilities. They believe in everyone's potential to reach astounding limits, yet they know those great feats begin with a few halting steps. A Learning Ally knows how to make those first few steps look possible, and motivates young people to take them.

A Learning Ally motivates by being a good model. The first step is to believe in yourself. You must believe you have something to offer and demonstrate your conviction by acting confidently when your student asks for help.

You must also demonstrate that belief by acting when they don't ask you. This means foreseeing the needs they might have for help and providing them opportunities to gain skill they never knew they needed. In this sense a Learning Ally is like a coach, but much less directive.

Kids are delighted by adults who believe in themselves. They are drawn to people who recognize their own skill and accomplishments. Even more, they admire people who know they have limitations but barge right ahead anyway. After all, this is the situation kids most often find themselves in.

This book is a formula for becoming a Learning Ally.

It doesn't take a lot of education, or a lot of guts, or even a lot of time. It does take a simple belief in yourself and a willingness to help another person do the same. If you can do that, the possibilities are endless.

A Story to Illustrate:

You have just found out that a friend and coworker you've known since childhood is functionally illiterate!

He can't read anything except the most simple words and phrases. Somehow he slipped through the cracks at school and has been faking it all these years. Due to a new assignment at work, your friend has become panicky about his lack of reading ability and has come to you for help.

You are shocked and embarrassed for him. You wonder how in the world something like this could happen. You can only imagine all the moments of hell he must have endured over the years. Then you're angry. It's all so senseless and cruel. Somebody should have helped your friend.

Probably you'd think all of these things and more. I would guess, though, that you'd spend little time worrying about whose fault it is that your friend failed to learn to read. After all, who cares whose fault it is? Your friend may have had a learning disability or been a distracted student. He may have attended an underfunded or poorly staffed school. There could be many explanations, but at this moment your concern is most likely to start fixing the problem, not the blame.

Immediately you say something reassuring. You make your friend feel better about himself, and help him see that many others have been in similar straits and have taken action to improve their abilities. You know the last thing to do is to blame him, because blaming only creates shame and anger, two things your friend probably has a lot of already.

You also know you can't do the learning for him. But you can share what you know and assist him in getting the information and help he's been too ashamed or timid to ask for. He needs your guidance and support more than he needs you to provide all the answers. So you're primarily interested in maintaining his self-esteem while steering him in the direction of learning opportunities.

This book will help you take the same approach toward the young people in your life. My intent is to aid you in casting off the rigid roles that are often foisted upon parents and guardians, and allow you to adopt the role of a Learning Ally.

My Story:

I came to write this book because I am profoundly concerned about the education of young people. I see far too many falling through the cracks of the system, family, and society.

I, too, was one of those kids. Midway through my senior year of high school, things began to fall apart. It became clear to me (and even worse, clear to my family) that I wouldn't be graduating. Although I'd never been a scholastic thunderhead, I had pulled C's and D's often enough to pass. Now a string of failing grades had caught up to me and the combined effect threatened my prospects of graduating. I found myself in a strangely pleasant environment. It seemed as though my lack of initiative had put me in control of a situation for the first time in my short life. Here was my whole family in a total dither. It had never been necessary to help in the education of my sister or brother, and my parents were at a loss as to how to help me. Worse yet, I seemed singularly unwilling to help myself and vaguely amused by the whole process.

"The truth is more important than the facts."

Frank Lloyd Wright

In the end I was saved by the combined efforts of a friendly cousin (my first and only Learning Ally) who taught school in the district and garnered support for me on the part of his colleagues, and my own motivation, fueled by the realization that I was the only one among my friends (no cabal of academic achievers here) who would not be graduating in the spring. I finally made it out the door with a grade point average hovering right around the one-point mark.

I recount this story not to dramatize my humble academic origins, but to highlight the need to support young people. Many kids today are just like I was, totally unprepared for the challenges of an education and desperately in need of a helping hand. And like me, they might not even know they are suffering. They might think things are just fine, or at least try to convince you they do.

I wrote this book so they can get the support I got 30 years ago. I wrote it so fewer kids might fall through the cracks. In today's world there are no nets! More than any other time in our history, kids need the assistance of adults who are willing to collaborate in their education.

I have been teaching all of my adult life. I'm very good at it, yet I didn't start out as a good teacher. I started out as a beginner, a learner, a wide-eyed student teacher with more idealism than knowledge. In my first full year of teaching, I taught next door to one of the best teachers I've ever seen. While I struggled to keep up with the basic curriculum, she had her class doing creative and exciting lessons that motivated and stimulated each and every student. One day when I was particularly down on myself, I pulled her aside and confided that I wondered if I could ever be as good a teacher as she was. It seemed as if she did everything right and I— well, I did everything wrong. Instead of responding with the sympathy I thought I needed, she gave me some advice for which I'll be forever grateful.

"Terry, you don't get it, do you?" she said.

"What do you mean," I stammered, shocked that I wasn't getting my tender ego stroked.

"You think that someone, somewhere, is doing it right, and you are doing it wrong, don't you?" she scolded me.

"Well, yeah I do, just look at your class . . ."

"Shut up about my class," she shot back, and pulled me away

from the rest of the teachers in the break room. She whispered, "I'm here to tell you a secret about teachers. The secret is that ***nobody's doing it right!*** Not one person here, not you, not them, not even me, is doing it right. What we're all doing is ***the best we can.*** If you insist on trying to do it right, you're gonna fail, because nobody can do that. If you focus on doing the best that Terry Mallen can, you'll be OK!"

My faith in my "best" wasn't so solid at that moment, but as I pondered her comments, a weight seemed to be lifted from my shoulders. If I really believed her, I wouldn't have to be looking around all the time comparing myself to my experienced counterparts. Doing my best made room for a mistake now and then. It made me realize that I wouldn't always do the right thing for every kid, and if I ever wanted to be an excellent teacher I would have to learn to live with that. Not accept it, mind you, but live with it as a reality of my profession.

Over the years I never stopped observing my peers, but I did quit obsessing over what I saw. I borrowed from the best with pride, and tried to avoid the mistakes I saw them make. I analyzed my own performance even more closely, recognizing that my own errors were at times hard to undo, and that the only restitution was in never repeating them again.

In the same manner, being a Learning Ally means doing ***the best you can.*** Recognize that you may not be the perfect person to help your youngster, but go ahead and do it anyway. Use this book to guide you and take the steps that will surely pay off for a child in your life.

How to Use This Book:

I've organized this book in a logical order, from the most fundamental and primary activities to those that could be considered supplemental. Each section stands alone and can be applied without regard to those that come before or after.

I don't know exactly the challenges you are facing with your young person, so I've tried to "cover the waterfront" with my advice. I'm confident, though, that your choices and common sense will prevail.

Pick through the book in any fashion you choose. My organization may not be yours. Treat it like a smorgasbord of tantalizing ideas. Start with dessert first if you wish. Dart around, picking only those things that seem tasty. Or begin at the beginning.

Of course, the advantage of a smorgasbord is that you can take a lot or a little, depending on your appetite. The same is true of these materials. Yet there is a difference. Here it's OK to sample something and then put it back. The trick is to try a lot of things so that you can see what works best for you and your young person. The more new ideas you tackle, the better your chances for success.

A LEARNING ALLY CHECKLIST

This book is for you if:

❏ You have some hopes and dreams for your kid.

❏ You consider yourself a pretty good person in most respects, but this schoolwork hassle is making you wonder if you've got the mettle.

❏ Secretly you know you were no better at doing your schoolwork than your kid, and you're afraid they'll spot you as a phoney.

❏ You were a near-perfect student. You were challenged by the work and loved your teachers. For the life of you, you just don't understand what the big deal is, and you're afraid your kid will perceive you as being "holier than thou."

❏ School was a hit-and-miss affair with you. Somehow you muddled through, but were rarely excited by anything that went on. You did make it through, but don't have much energy to do it all over again with your child.

❏ You've met with your student's teacher, but feel that little was accomplished. (You were forced to sit in one of those miniature desks!)

❏ You want to give your kid constructive criticism, but it always comes out "destructive crudacism."

❏ You actually start avoiding your kid to cut down on conflicts. You can't deal with another argument.

❏ Sometimes you use too much firepower and sometimes too little. Your body language sends a different message than your words.

You've got what it takes to be a Learning Ally if:

❑ You've ever been so proud of your kid that you could burst.

❑ You have some hopes and dreams for your kid.

❑ You have a great desire to help your kid, but find him strangely resistant to your efforts.

❑ Sometime, somewhere, in some situation, another person told you that you have patience. (One instance is sufficient to qualify you for Learning Allyhood!)

❑ You love your kid and want to help her with her studies.

❑ You are willing to stop doing stuff that isn't effective.

❑ You're willing to invest a little more time.

❑ You are willing to try some new things (even if they're a little awkward at times).

❑ You want to see some great improvement and enjoy yourself in the process.

❑ You still have that "sense of wonder," but sometimes wonder where it went to in your kid.

Take Charge:

Stop Doing
What Doesn't Work

This book is about doing simple, effective things to help your young person succeed in school.

I've made every effort to be positive and focus my advice on constructive, affirmative approaches. There are, however, some things that are fundamentally non-constructive. You, the Learning Ally, should stop doing them right now! Once you've stopped doing all the things you're presently doing that don't work, you'll have all kinds of time to try the constructive alternatives in this book that do work.

Stop Waiting for Schools to Get Better

If you've been thinking that the shortcomings in your school system have something to do with your student's difficulty, you're probably right. Most schools are having a rough time of it. Our system was designed for a country that has long since passed. It takes a massive amount of creativity for teachers and administrators just to avoid meltdown!

It's no secret. Everyone knows the educational system needs revamping. The president, local politicians, and even students are seen on TV making comments on the need for improvement. Consequently you get the impression that those changes, those improvements must be right around the corner—just in time for your kid. It's an erroneous impression.

The system will not improve in time for your kid! It won't happen fast enough. Change in any large bureaucracy just doesn't happen that rapidly. There are too many roadblocks. There is too much vested interest in the status quo. The improvements will be gradual and conservative.

So quit waiting! You must do some things today that will make up for the failings of the educational system. Waiting for others to do what is required only means the shop will be closed by the time it's your kid's turn.

Stop Screaming, Nagging, Pleading, and Preaching

We often get backed into a corner with kids. We don't have a lot of alternatives to the way we're handling them.

Everyone does the best they can.

When that best effort fails, we're stuck. In the absence of any better ideas, we tend to fall back on the same old approaches. We try the same stuff again, only louder and more frequently. In the end we get the same old results. But as a wise person once said:

"If you always do what you've always done, you'll always get what you've always got!"

So if you've been yelling and screaming at your kids, stop it! If you've been nagging, prodding, scolding them, stop it! If you've been doing your kid's work for them, stop it! If you've been begging and pleading with them, stop it right now! It's useless! It doesn't work and it makes both of you feel rotten. Whatever you've been doing that hasn't worked, simply cease and desist. All you are accomplishing is hassling your kid and teaching them how to ignore you.

Stop Judging
Your Young Person Based on Their
Achievement in School

"But," you say, "I don't do that! They know I'm only coming down hard on them for their own good. I tell them all the time how much they mean to me . . . how much I love them."

I'm going to tell you right out: **They don't hear you!** They don't get your message. They don't make the distinction between "your work stinks" and "*you* stink."

No matter how careful you are, no matter how articulate you are, they won't get the message you are sending when you say, "Your

school work is terrible, but you, as a person, are just fine." All they hear is a negative judgment of them as a person, and it feels terrible. Young people who feel terrible about themselves have a hard time doing their best work.

Once you are convinced of this, you'll change the way you talk to your young person about their work. You'll stop judging them based on their performance, and they'll be free to do their best because they know, in your eyes, they are the best.

This is true even when their performance falls short.

You can still talk to them about it. You can still find out what went wrong, but you need to be skillful.

The key here is to get them to say it! Ask them questions about the work. If it's a failed test or an incomplete assignment, say, "Hmm, how do you feel about this, Tim?" Let Tim characterize it. He knows it's a lousy job. He doesn't need you to remind him. In fact, he'll resent you for it—and he should. None of us likes to have our nose rubbed in our failure. We want someone who'll listen to our gripes and then help us find a way to improve.

So when Tim responds, "I don't know, crappy, I guess. What'm I s'posed to feel? Proud?" you can pause, take a breath and say, "Yeah, I guess you're right, proud probably isn't the best emotion to connect with this test. But let's look at the situation. How did you end up staring at a big F in math?"

In this way you *concentrate on the situation, event, or assignment, and not on your student.* They will put enough blame on themselves!

Stop judging, not because you don't care, but because it's the only way you can position yourself as a Learning Ally. It's the only way you can quit being someone who wants to *fix the blame* and become someone who wants to *fix the problem!*

Stop Giving the Benefit of the Doubt to Educators

Teachers and administrators are not the enemy. They are committed, hardworking people. Even so, you must assume that you, not they, are always right. The playing field on which parents and schools interact is not level. The odds are stacked in favor of the system's needs, not yours. As I see it, this is just the reverse of what it should be.

Level that playing field by always giving **yourself** the benefit of the doubt! Begin by assuming you are right in whatever you think or believe about your young person. After all, **you are the customer!** That's right, parents and students are the primary **customers** of the educational system. Too often they've been treated like outsiders, and that's simply wrong.

A lot of us have a bad habit of deferring to certain authorities when it's not called for. This is especially true when we deal with educators. We automatically tend to be shy, retiring, and hesitant.

During our own schooldays we were rightly taught to respect "the teacher." In many cases this included never contradicting what they had to say. We were trained to take, at face value, everything teachers said. We called those things facts, and we learned it didn't often pay to dispute our teacher's findings.

Today that very reticence to challenge educational authority may contribute to your young person's failure. Remember that you aren't a kid anymore! You're a fully grown adult who has life experiences, convictions, and knowledge to offer. You can be confident in the value of these offerings. You needn't defer to the teacher or principal, especially when you are working on behalf of your young person.

Give yourself the benefit of the doubt! Make the schools demonstrate that your assumptions are off-base before you accept theirs. Deprive them of the benefit of the doubt, and insist they substantiate what they believe about your kid. Don't do this out of disrespect. Do it out of necessity. Do it because you know that the school's need for authority and control often conflicts with the learning needs of your student! *It's true that you may not always be right, but you're always the customer!*

2

Take Charge

By Being Positive

Put on those rose-colored glasses.

Don't wait for your youngster to get all fired up about education. As a Learning Ally, set the tone for them by taking positive, constructive action that makes it clear you expect success and have every confidence they are capable of it. Reward their progress richly and let them know you're impressed. Bolster their resolve with a gentle hand, and portray the ultimate payoff with all the colors of your palette.

Assume They Have a "Good" Reason for Everything They Do

Rationale: An assumption worth taking a risk on is that young people have valid reasons for everything they do.

I recognize that this flies in the face of conventional logic. We all know that kids just "do stuff." Their actions aren't planned. Most of the time **they** can't even predict their behavior! What they do seems to be no more than chemistry or chance variation.

By contrast we perceive adults as prudent, well advised and sensible. But is this true?

"A child's wisdom is also wisdom."

Yiddish Proverb

I'm reminded of the story of the man who ran naked through the cactus patch. When he emerged on the other side with thousands of painful punctures, someone asked him why he had done it. To which he replied, "It seemed like a good idea at the time!"

If you're like most people, there are a lot of events in your own life that can only be explained with the same "naked man's" rationale. As adults we often don't have the best reasons for our behavior, either. We surely don't expect to explain it all. We just accept responsibility to make things right. At work we don't go around demanding justification from adults every time their behavior puzzles us. We assume they have their reasons and find ways to work with the situation. So where's the sense in treating kids any differently? Why saddle them with the burden of consistent, sound judgment?

Of course, kids do make decisions differently than adults. They use "kid logic," which is more fluid than the adult counterpart. It's rapid. It's focused on the here and now, and makes sense out of a universe populated only by themselves. Alone they make judgments about what is reasonable. They're not encumbered by concerns of family, community, or future. There's only "this moment" in all its immediate glory.

A Learning Ally recognizes this fundamental difference in world view. Instead of attacking the youngster's inherent selfishness, the Ally honors it and accepts it as a point along the way, a necessary phase in the development of a fully responsible set of values. Failure in this effort only arrests that development and produces the very outcome the adult is trying to avoid.

Assuming that kids have a "good" reason for the things they do allows you to see their behavior clearly. You're not burdened with endless ruminations about their motives and goals. You don't have to waste a lot of time sweating the real story out of them. You can get right to the crux of the issue, because your attitude doesn't make them defensive. They don't feel compelled to explain why they ran naked through the cactus. Instead they can get to the relevant issue more quickly. And that is to ask for your help.

How To Do It: Don't waste time being baffled by your kid's behavior. You aren't stuck with the negative visions you may now have. Replace them with positive, constructive images that honor your kid's intellect.

1. On a daily basis, look at your young person and say something like this to yourself: "Now here is a kid who takes a thoughtful and reasoned approach to life. She makes decisions that are logical and strategic based on the data she has." It doesn't matter if you believe it or not; just say it to yourself at least once every day. The benefits will accrue as your young person gradually begins to react to the positive impression they see reflected in you!

You might jot your positive statement down on a 3x5 card. On the back add some disclaimers if you want:

▲ The data my kid finds valid and the data I find valid may often differ. This is not wrong, just factual.

▲ My values and my kid's values will not necessarily be the same. This is not wrong, just factual.

▲ I needn't approve of my kid's decisions to be of service. My goal is to help and support, not to judge.

Once you've altered your assumptions by choosing to see your young person in this fashion, it'll be easier to carry out the second step in this process.

2. Whenever you want to ask why your kid did something (especially an action that completely baffles you in its ignorance and stupidity), *stop!* Replace questions about motives with offers of help.

Doing this frees you from a futile search for blame. More important, it sends the message to your young person that you respect him. In most cases it allows him the breathing space to tell you the "why," anyway.

So instead of screaming, "What in the world would possess you to run naked through a patch of cactus?" Learning Allies would say something like this: "Ouch, I bet that hurts! Is there something I can do to help you?" (While all the time thinking the aforementioned question. After all, Learning Allies are human!)

Your punctured progeny looks up at you in a moment of stunned silence. "Uh, I've got a long story to tell you, Dad, but first, do you have a bathrobe and some bandages?"

Pitfalls: To assume logic on the part of your young person may require a gigantic leap of faith for some of you. The only way to succeed is to take it!

You needn't be a believer from the outset. Continue to reaffirm your assumptions by looking at your kid and saying to yourself, "This kid has got it together!" Say it with conviction and fervor. Don't let the fact that the statement doesn't agree with reality stop you. Changes of this nature often require that people suspend their perception of reality.

Gradually you'll begin to feel that it's true, and that's the first step toward progress. Your young person will see this and respond positively. They perceive feelings much more clearly than they do knowledge. If you *feel* it, they will *see* it!

Look at it this way. What's easier? To change the way your kid operates in the world or to change the way you see things? In one option you only have some control, and in the other full control. The choice is simple and the process even simpler. Don't let the challenge of a little illusion stop you.

Catch Them Doing Right

Rationale: The object of effective praise is to "catch" your kid doing something right! Having caught them, you then do something to reinforce the appropriate behavior. Young people often don't know what appropriate behavior is. It's hard for them to "see" their own success. They need your help in identifying those things that are worthy of repetition. You can provide that help by giving frequent, enthusiastic praise.

Nothing in your kid's life is more positive and rewarding than your approval. Everything they do, in one way or another, is an attempt to get this approval. Being ready and willing to give it is one of the most important things you can do.

"But," you say, "my kid couldn't care less about me or my approval. She's only interested in her friends, music, and that godawful skateboard!"

Don't believe it! It's a smoke screen. She just doesn't know how to tell you how much she wants your approval and admiration.

Sure, kids have other interests. They don't come running to you with every accomplishment or every problem they have in school. More and more they need their peers. They look to friends to provide a mirror, to get a sense of who they are. Friends are important in the overall development of a young person. A kid needs friends, but needs you even more.

As they mature, it might look as if young people have outgrown the need for a pat on the head, but they still yearn for your reassurance and confidence. Friends can't supply this precious commodity. Only you can.

A powerful Learning Ally uses praise as part of a strategy to build their young person's self-confidence and to reinforce productive behavior. Even in the face of resistance and apparent apathy, a Learning Ally will continue to give frequent and appropriate praise, and will assure the young person that good work and improvement are taking place. There is nothing more effective in fueling a young persons's achievement than to earn and receive the praise of the adults in her life!

I'M PROUD OF YOU! NICE! WORK WAY!! TO GOOD GO YOU! HAVE! TALENT HON!

How To Do It: Catching your kid doing something right and praising her effectively is relatively simple. It will require a little research, some planning, and much discipline on your part. But the payoff is immediate and powerful.

1. Figure out what kind of praise works for your kid.

Does your kid appreciate dramatics? Would she be pleased if you went dancing into the streets with her report card? Would she enjoy it if you carved her grade point average into the lawn? Maybe a tasteful, full-page rendition of the last progress report, published in the Sunday Supplement of your local newspaper, would fit the bill.

Or is your kid more private? Does she like a low-key hug and a whispered "Nice going!" Would she really enjoy some quiet time with you? Possibly an afternoon outing or a dinner would be just the thing.

We're all different, thank goodness. But that uniqueness makes your job more difficult. Praise that works for one kid will not work for another.

If you're working with your own child or a child you know well, you probably sense already what they're comfortable with, what "pushes their buttons." Even so, try some of the different approaches I'll suggest. It never hurts to mix it up. At worst they'll think you're a little weird, and that's not all bad, either!

2. Be specific in your praise.

Once you've figured out what will work with your young person, you'll want to plan to make the praise as effective as possible. You'll want to avoid making trite remarks that accomplish just the opposite of what you are attempting. Praise that works is specific. It describes—in a detailed fashion—just what it is about the person or their work that deserves recognition:

"Hey, that looks great, Katie! When you turn in work that's as neat and organized as that, you can't help but get a good grade. Have you ever considered being an engineer?"

It often helps if you ask a question that lets the person expand on what they've done. This lets them give you even more specifics about their handiwork:

"Wow, that's some drawing! Y' know, it's not just lines, all those shaded areas really give it a three-dimensional look! How'd you figure out where to put the shadows?"

"Uh, well, I don't know where I learned about the shading. It just looked right. I guess I've seen it on other drawings. It really looks real, huh?"

"You bet it does! Well, I guess it just means you're a natural artist."

Believing that you are a "natural" makes anything much easier to learn! I use this kind of question and comment with a lot of young people. It rarely fails to make them proud of themselves, and I always feel genuine in my praise because, in truth, we are all "naturals" if we'd give ourselves half a chance! When you are trying to be specific in your praise, think, "What is it about this work or performance that is especially well done? What shows some real improvement, or demonstrates a skill that they can continue to use and refine?"

You needn't sum up all their good work in one profoundly rewarding statement. It's not possible, and they won't believe you anyway. Just look for something you find impressive and jump on it.

"You're pretty handy with that dictionary. I've noticed you looked up two words in the last five minutes. You know, using the dictionary that effectively is a great habit to develop."

The more you practice, the easier it'll get. You'll be increasingly specific about what you are praising, and you'll do it in a relaxed and genuine way. Remember, being precise about what you are admiring makes you believable.

On the other hand, it doesn't hurt, every once in a while, to say something general and off-the-wall, like:

"Have I told you recently what a fine person you are? You make the world a better place to live in."

Try it. It's fun to see how they react.

3. Praise often.

In order to figure out what works for your kid and develop the ability to be specific, you must discipline yourself. Discipline is necessary because without it most of us fail to praise often enough to have a "strategic" effect. It just becomes a nice thing that happens, rather than the fuel that propels your youngster to their best efforts.

For one reason or another, it's difficult for most of us to cut loose with a lot of compliments. It seems like so much fluff. Either we're afraid of being phoney or we really don't trust the value of praise.

Maybe we received very little praise as a young person ourselves, so heaping it on someone else seems a lot like indulgence. It could be we're afraid that it'll encourage the kid to sit back on their laurels if we praise them too lavishly. Who knows why, but it's hard to be consistent and prolific with praise. The question is, what should you do to counteract this natural tendency to be so miserly with compliments?

The answer is to be disciplined! Put yourself on a regime. Commit yourself to catching your kid doing things right, every day. Be ready to pounce on commendable behavior at a moment's notice, and rely on your skills in specificity to make it believable.

Commit to a number! Decide how many compliments you want to give your young person in a week or a day, and then see if you follow through. Start with one. It's as good a place to start as any. See if you can do it. See if you can catch your young person doing one thing right, at least once a day.

Another way to become disciplined is to look at the amount of praise you give your young person in relation to criticism. A good ratio is three to one. You should be praising them three times for every time you criticize them. That's three "atta-boys" or "atta-girls" for every "ah-shoot."

You may have to keep count at first. Make notes on your performance. Put pluses and minuses on a notepad somewhere so you can tell if you're really maintaining an effective level of praise. Once you get the 3:1 ratio, work on refining your praise. Customize it, make it more specific, and ask probing insightful questions that let your kid "strut her stuff!" Remember, we're all naturals at accepting specific, genuine, praise!

> "He that bringeth the present findeth the door open."
>
> Thomas Fuller, MD

Pitfalls: Kids are often great actors. Don't let them convince you that your praise has no impact. Don't fall for this con. They are desperately concerned about what you think! And they profoundly need your approval. Some of them don't know it. Others just won't admit it.

It's strange that kids react this way. I think it's natural, though. Kids need your guidance and nurturing, and at the same time need to cast off your influence and try to make it on their own. The good news is, you don't need to understand their motives to deal effectively with the situation.

Your role is to behave as if you are the most important person in their world (by the way, you are!) Your confidence will be infectious, and they'll buy into the assumption that their highest goal is to make you proud of them. Don't lose faith! Your calm sense of purpose and direction will be irresistible.

Reward the Constructive Things

Rationale: We are all more apt to continue doing things we are rewarded for. Conversely, we are less likely to repeat things that get neutral or punishing responses. It's as simple as that.

So why are we all so squeamish when it comes to rewarding our kids for doing the right thing at school?

Many adults think it's not fair. They think students should apply themselves and learn as much as they can because it's good for them. "It's their duty!" these adults say. "Heck, it's not like they work or anything. Most of them don't even do their chores half the time. Working hard at school is the least they can do in light of everything they get from the adults in their lives. They should put their noses to the grindstone and scrape off some flesh, not concern themselves with rewards."

Unfortunately, it's the rare kid who sees it that way. Most of them ask the basic question, silently if not openly, "What's in it for me?"

Your job is to set aside your judgments, find "what's in it for them," and deliver it when they successfully meet their goals. Learning Allies are well armed with significant payoffs. They deliver the goods when kids do things worthy of repetition, like completing their work on time, reading on a regular basis, or raising their marks in geometry.

There is sound reason behind "bribing" kids. It makes sense to create a habit now that is driven by a tangible personal reward. It makes sense because that habit will continue on its own merits long after you stop with the money, the toys, and the car keys.

How To Do It:

1. Determine together what the rewards will be.

      Begin your process of rewarding by finding out what your youngster values. Ask them what they feel would be fair for achieving certain goals you both set.

    Kids will often talk in terms of money or free time or access to the family car. But the most effective reward of all is something only you can provide and they probably won't ask for: your undivided attention and approval. These are the highest, most valuable gifts you can give them. Kids are just too self-conscious to tell you this. So agree to the trinkets they think they want, while vowing to yourself that you will supply the real, heavy-duty payoff of your own personal attention and acceptance.

2. Determine together what to reward.

Negotiate rewards for the full spectrum of activities that you both agree are key to their success, such as reading books, finishing homework, or improving test scores. Make sure you are recognizing both short-and long-term achievement as well as mixing up difficult and routine tasks.

3. When your kid earns it, give both the tangible reward you agreed on and the intangible, more important reward of yourself.

Pitfalls: Every kid is an entrepreneur. They're tough businesspeople and will take you for everything you've got if you don't watch out.

Be firm and get them in on the act. Make sure they are involved in determining what "appropriate" rewards are. Appeal to their sense of fair play. They won't often let you down. If you do sense you're being asked to reward activities that are less than challenging, tell them. It does no good to institute a process of reinforcements that end up being awards for merely living and breathing.

Don't reward everything. Your main targets are areas that need improvement and areas where you want to reinforce continued solid work.

Don't reward them when they don't deserve it. You are doing them a great disservice when you do. You reinforce the notion that they can get something for nothing. It's hard for either of you to take pride in that kind of folly.

Having clear goals that are specific, measurable, and timed make this less likely. When milestones of this nature are met, it's easy for both of you to agree that they've earned their payoff.

Express Your Admiration

Rationale: Every young person should know they are admired by an adult in their life.

Being the focus of another person's genuine admiration is a powerful elixir. It convinces you, in the strongest way, that you are a person of substance. You've done something worthy of their admiration, maybe even a bit of envy.

Admiration differentiates you from the crowd. It helps you see yourself as a unique human being unlike any other. At the same time a bond is built between two people. The seed is planted for the inevitable mutual admiration that will grow. The very best relationships between young learners and their Learning Allies are characterized by this kind of shared positive regard.

Young people who have the admiration of an adult in their life find it easy to believe in themselves. They can rely on the firm support of their not-so-secret admirer, even when their own resolve and self-esteem are shaken. This firm foundation of personal worth helps a youngster "hang in there" when things get rough. They manage to do this because they can draw on faith that even they don't have. They can tap the resources of the person who admires them.

How To Do It:

1. Find specific abilities to admire.

Go on a search for those things that your young person can do that you genuinely admire. It's OK to admire them as a person in general, but that's not specific enough. You need to identify definite skills and abilities they have that are worthy of your admiration.

2. Express your admiration in an effective way.

Once you've found an ability or two that are prime targets for your admiration, make certain you express yourself in a way that your youngster can believe. Let's say you think they are especially gifted at drawing and painting, and you would like to say something that expresses your admiration for the time and effort they put into their artwork. You might say something like this:

"Hmmm, darned if that doesn't look like a horse. Sure don't know where you got that ability. Must've been from your mom's side of the family."

This comment does send the message of admiration, but in an ambiguous way. It betrays the giver's uneasiness with just saying directly that they admire their young person's ability. If they took a moment and planned to communicate their admiration effectively, the comment might sound something like this:

"Whoa! That's a beautiful horse, Tanya! You know I've always wished I could draw like that. I really admire you. You've spent the time and energy to learn to draw a horse that looks life-like. It must feel good to be that artistic."

As Tanya's head begins to swell uncontrollably, let's examine why this second comment is so effective. It meets three criteria of a good "admiration statement" by stating:

▲ What is worthy of admiration (a beautifully drawn horse)

▲ Why you admire them ("I've always wished I could draw. . .")

▲ Provides an opening for them to expand ("It must feel . . .")

Remember, you admire **people,** based on specific things they say and do. Always include the phrase, ***"I admire you."*** It's the simplest way to say it.

Some other examples are:

"I noticed how you helped resolve the fight between Dale and Kit. I really admire that ability in you. It takes real guts to jump in and offer your help. Myself, I've always been afraid the war-ring parties would just tell me to take a leap. Aren't you ever worried about a reaction like that?"

"I can live for two months on a good compliment."

Mark Twain

"Unbelievable! Wendy, you crunch those numbers like a computer, yet you make it look like an art. I admire you. I work like a dog and can't seem to balance my checkbook. Was it always as enjoyable and simple as you make it look?"

"That was wonderful, Alex! I can't believe you've only been playing the piano for a year! You seem like a natural, but I bet it's more a case of natural work and discipline. I admire you. You have real tenacity. I wish I would have done the same. What keeps you playing and practicing?"

Communicating your admiration will take a bit of planning, and maybe even some practice with another person or a mirror. In the end, you'll be able to directly and effectively deliver a statement that lets your young person know she is a formidable person, of admirable qualities.

Pitfalls: Keep things in perspective. Don't overdo the admiration or your credibility will suffer. It's best to test the waters, be a bit conservative at first, and then build to a chest-bursting crescendo. The other way around makes everyone feel awkward.

Don't fake it! You can't fool kids. If you don't see anything to admire at the moment, don't try to make something up. Look harder or work with your young person until they are achieving at a level worthy of your admiration, and then give it to them.

Admiration is something we earn. It shouldn't be confused with the basic, positive regard and respect the Learning Ally has for their young person. Young people get this kind of support just because they are special people to you. They don't need to earn it. They do need to earn your admiration.

Connect Hard Work with a Future Payoff

Rationale: I saw a poster the other day that summed up this issue very well. It showed an aerial view of a beautiful California beach mansion. Jutting from the darkness of a six-car garage were the tail sections of various Ferraris, Porsches, and Mercedes Benzes. The caption below the photo read: "The Value of Higher Education!"

You might argue that there are loftier goals than financial excess to which your young person should aspire, and I would agree. Yet the poster makes an intense and immediate point—work and discipline now, pay off in comfort and security later. This is true whether your goal is spiritual harmony or a sixty-foot yacht.

The payoff your student is working for should be just as clear and dramatic. The reasons for investing time and energy in study should never be foggy.

Kids who are convinced that they have a rosy future behave according to that belief. They work hard, they plan, and they make sacrifices to ensure that that future comes to pass.

Yet many kids are notoriously nearsighted. Long-range vision is rarely their strong suit. It's hard enough for them to imagine the end of the day or week, let alone the completion of their education and entry into the world of work. Finding a way to connect their efforts today and tomorrow with the ultimate payoff years down the road is a real challenge. Learning Allies assist young people in making that connection.

Helping your young person see the future clearly can make the difference between a student who feels like a victim, simply tolerating the stress and anguish of education, and a kid who attacks each new assignment as another stepping stone bringing them closer to their goal. This attitude makes school an exciting journey rather than a trap.

You have the ability to see your young person's future. The images are all there: the good lifestyle, the health, and family joy. **Your challenge is in cramming that vision into their head!**

How To Do It:

1. Stop pontificating about their future.

It's impossible to cram *your* dreams into their heads! No matter how logical or accurate, the images in your mind cannot be planted into your kid's brain. The best you can do is support activities that help your young person create their own version of a future they want. If you do it right, they'll incorporate some of your vision as well.

The future is often a distant, foggy, even nonexistent, realm for kids. You can't sell it to them. You can't interpret it. They're resistant to your explanations. By the time most of them are school-aged, they've heard enough explanations for a lifetime. They don't want your impressions and predictions.

What they want and need is their own experience. Regardless of how illogical it is, they want to sample the future now, so they can determine whether it's worth working for. They want to see it and feel it and taste it, just to be sure.

2. Give them role models so they can see for themselves the rewards of hard work.

As a Learning Ally, your job is to provide the opportunity for your kid to see the connection between hard work and the future. Just like salespeople in the grocery store, a Learning Ally stands at the end of an aisle and hands out little sausages that represent the appetizing future that's in store for a diligent student. These tasty little samples of the "good life" are usually made up of opportunities to get very close to someone who has profited mightily from education.

This person could be a pharmacist, musician, or a game warden. It doesn't matter. What does matter is proximity. Provide an opportunity for your young person to encounter people who have done commendable things. Make sure they are close enough to get the scent of achievement all over them. Especially get them close to people who have achieved happiness and met their life goals through hard work and devotion to an arduous course of study.

It's not good enough to sit and watch. Young people have to be involved. They tire quickly of being spectators. They want to actually do something for once! Many young people get this opportunity to "do something" through helping or apprenticing themselves to a successful person.

This opportunity could take the form of helping out in a relative's business, volunteering to assist counselors at a summer camp, or even assisting you at your own place of work.

Now that would be a great place to begin! After all, who would be a better role model than you, the person who has decided to be their Learning Ally? Start by taking them to work with you and giving them something meaningful and productive to do. Then look for other opportunities to pair them with good role models. Think about who you admire at work. Would they be willing to spend a little time with your kid? Don't assume that all people are too busy or find this kind of mentoring an imposition. Many people would be highly complimented by your request.

It's best if your student has an interest in the person's field of endeavor, but not necessary. All good role models will display similar behaviors of commitment, hard work, and enjoyment. Just make sure your child has an opportunity to spend time, shoulder to shoulder, with a person who has actually profited from the hard work and study you want to reinforce. Start your search with yourself. You'd be great!

Pitfalls: Don't expect the people you are putting your kid in contact with to be instructors. It's enough that they be seen and heard as good role models. Proximity is more important than instruction. These people will be living examples of the rewards that await students who work hard and do well in school.

Don't Let Them Quit

Rationale: Quitting is a habit that starts early in life and stays around for a long time. Kids don't know how dangerous this habit is. They often see it as an accept-able, face-saving alternative when the going gets tough. In their minds, it's a lot better to have quit a "stupid" game or activity than to have been a failure.

In a way, quitting is proactive. The person who quits is taking what little control they have of the situation, and cutting their losses. "Hanging in there" and failing, on the other hand, seems to be asking for punishment. It's something they have little control over. The shame and humiliation of defeat is especially sharp in light of their helplessness.

Acute fear of failure drives the habit of quitting, not laziness. However, many adults see kids who have a habit of quitting exactly this way, as indolent and lazy. These adults pile on the shame and blame, never realizing the depth of their youngster's terror. Addressing your young person's quitting realistically, as a symptom of fear, opens many doors. Freed from the trap of judgment, you can intervene and help them finish what they begin.

"Winners never quit, quitters never win."

Kids often get started in activities or projects that rapidly get too challenging. Their immense enthusiasm quickly wanes when they find that, like most worthwhile endeavors, this one involves some tedium and work. And then they want to bail out! You, as their Learning Ally, will find yourself between a rock and a hard place. On one hand you don't want to see a habit of quitting develop. On the other, you know that if forced to continue, they are likely to do work that is less than their best. In a way, you'll be setting them up for failure, but that's just what you should do. ***Set them up to fail rather than to quit.*** Failure has been an integral part of the lives of all successful people. Quitting hasn't. Inoculate your youngster against this chronic disease of the spirit by helping them finish what they start.

One of the greatest lessons you can help your young person learn is that effort and tenacity are a reward in themselves. Praise them for hanging in there and completing what they start. Especially heap it on when other kids have far outstripped their performance. Make it worthwhile, even when they come in last.

How To Do It:

1.   Do everything in your power to assist your kid in finishing those things they start.

Help them use appropriate judgment in committing to projects, and help them foresee the massive effort that's often required to finish. Young people see the immediate situation and often the goal, but the middle, work-intensive steps are pretty foggy. Help them clearly see this "middle world" of effort and diligence. Don't scare them, but lay it all out so they are aware of the total challenge. In the end, even if you have to literally hover over them while they work—do it! Even if you end up helping them more than you want—do it! Finishing is far more important than winning.

2.   Tell them stories about how you've had to "hang in there" in your life.

Tell them how much it hurt, how hard it was, and then tell them how sweet the payoff was, whether or not you were victorious. Don't worry about being a braggart; kids know the difference between a genuine effort to share your life's lessons, and blowing your own horn. Your stories don't have to be dramatic, either. You needn't have climbed Everest or earned a Nobel prize to impress kids. The only requirement is to have "hung in there" long enough and tenaciously enough to see some real payoff in your life. The closer your story is to a real-life situation that they can relate to, the better.

3.   Expose them to the wealth of literature about people who've overcome great odds through perseverance and personal courage.

These are popular books with kids. Your librarian should be able to provide ten titles right off the tip of his tongue.

Pitfalls: Don't underestimate how quickly a habit like quitting can get started. Let nothing slide by. Make a stand on even the smallest projects. Always encourage and reward their best, most complete work.

Remember, the desire to quit is natural and at times makes some sense. Don't judge your young person harshly for wanting to take this option. Replace those sentiments of anger or disappointment with a desire to make the project possible. The magnitude of any assignment can often overwhelm a youngster. Your goodwill and support can make them feel confident and able once again.

Listen closely. Quitting can be a symptom of things going seriously wrong. If your youngster announces they are quitting choir or soccer or the pep club, resist the urge to respond immediately. Wait, take a breath, and give them enough time to tell you the whole story. There are those rare situations when it does make sense to call it quits.

They need your support then, too.

Take Charge

By Dealing Effectively With the Downside

The brightest, most cheery attitude won't stop the rain from coming down.

We all get wet once in a while. The trick is to avoid drowning in the downpour. Recognize that everyone, including you and your young person, come with a unique set of baggage. This set of bags is full of habits and ways of coping that are probably pretty threadbare, especially for inclement weather. Shop around in this chapter for some new survival gear, and then when things go wrong, as they inevitably will, you can deal effectively with the downside.

Eliminate Fear as a Tool of Motivation

Rationale: Some of you may be thinking that without the threat of doom, your young person would fail to do anything. In a way this may be true; kids who've had a steady diet of intimidation often have difficulty responding to more positive approaches. It's as though they're addicted to the fight-or-flight highs of producing under pressure.

"What we fear comes to pass more speedily than what we hope."

Publilius Syrus

We all have life experiences that support the contention that fear is a great motivator. A whole lot of our learning has been the direct result of terror. In fact, some of us feel we learn best with threats hanging over our head. There's no doubt about it: fear works! It gets us off our duffs. It shatters our complacency. There's a problem with learning this way. When we learn fearfully, we also learn to hate. If we're lucky we just end up hating poetry or geometry. Think of all the people who have spent years learning to play musical instruments that they now refuse to even touch. If we're unlucky we generalize our bad feelings to the teacher, the school, and the whole process of education. Given the choice, we're less likely to return to the learning environment. Many people will simply cut their losses and run.

Kids who hate don't have too much trouble expressing it. They simply say things like, "I can't stand Mr. Mallen. He's the worst teacher I've ever had!"

Or they say, "This is such a jerky school. I'm not gonna go anymore. I wish I was back at my old school. At least there they treated you like a person and everyone wasn't weird!" The most serious side-effect of fearful learning occurs when the student turns the hate and frustration back on *themselves.* They blame and despise themselves for a situation they had no hand in creating. In the end they feel like helpless, intimidated pawns. They don't say much about what they hate anymore. Why bother?

It's no wonder kids react this way. Nobody likes to feel scared and out of control. And that's just how it feels when someone scares us into learning new things.

Motivating with fear is dangerous.

Its side-effects are bad for your kid. Fear causes:

anger
stress
fatigue
anxiety
depression
self-doubt
low self-esteem
inaction
finger-pointing
refusal to take risks
refusal to take responsibility
low creativity
quitting

As a Learning Ally it's important that you totally eliminate fear from your bag of motivational tools. Give up on it and start building skills that support your young learner in a stable, friendly environment. Even if you don't replace fear with something more positive, the absence of threat itself will support better achievement.

The payoff far outweighs the extra effort. Kids who learn without fear actually enjoy the process. They retain more of the material, and the best part is, they always come back for more!

How To Do It:

1. The first step is to collect some data. Find out what you are now doing that is producing fearful reactions in your young person. Ask *them* what you are presently doing that is threatening. Tell them you want to know so you can stop. Be straightforward and direct about your motives. A Learning Ally always makes it clear why they are collecting data and what they are going to do with it. That way young learners can be as free as possible in supplying the information needed.

The answers you get will probably be like these:

▲ "Stop warning me about the gloom and doom that awaits if I don't start applying myself."

▲ "Stop threatening to punish me if I don't get better grades."

▲ "Stop threatening to inform on me!" (As in, you're gonna tell Dad or Mom or Uncle Ralph)

▲ "Stop asking leading questions that begin with, 'How do you expect to . . .'"

▲ "Stop telling me tales of woe regarding other young people who failed to work up to their potential."

▲ "Stop reminding me about how important it is to get in the right schools."

▲ "Stop fretting and giving me the silent treatment."

2. The next step is to actually stop doing what your kid has told you is threatening. Instead remind them of their goals and point out how their present activity is going to pay off.

This may cause a little discomfort for a while. You'll feel as if you have no ammunition, nothing substantial to influence them with. But you do, and it's even more powerful than fear.

Be proactive. Don't wait until your kid does something that would normally cause you to threaten them. Catch them before they have a chance to mess up and point out how their present performance will ultimately pay off.

You might say something like:

"I noticed you sat right down and went to work on your homework today. That's the kind of devotion to your work that can't help but earn an A in math. Nice job, Shannon!"

If your kid does do something that has dire academic consequences, ***stop! Do nothing!*** Leave the room if necessary, but don't revert to your old practice of motivating with fear. Take a few moments to collect your thoughts, and plan to say or do something that is a positive reaction to this negative situation. Often this can be a simple open-ended question like, ***"OK, Todd, you got a D on this quiz. What do you think it'll do to your goal of getting a C+ this term?"***

Notice that this question is a lot like, "How do you expect to raise your grade if you keep getting D's on your quizzes?" Yet it is different. The positive reaction asks for more information. The threatening question requires Todd to justify his behavior. Gather data, don't demand explanations!

Pitfalls: If you find yourself falling back into bad habits of motivating with fear, simply "erase" your words and start over.

Let's say you just received a call from your young person's physics teacher. It seems that your kid's portion of a group project is three days late. The teacher is worried that your kid will fail as well as demoralize her project team. You politely assure him that action will be taken. You slam the phone down, march into her room and say,

"Lori, I just got a call from Mr. Lever. If you don't get that project done, there'll be no license, no car, and no social life. Do you understand me?"

Before she has a chance to respond, stop and erase your words. Say, *"No, that's not what I wanted to say. My goal is to help you, not threaten you."*

These words will effectively defuse your negative comment and give you the opportunity to react in a constructive fashion by saying something like,

"What I want to say is . . . Lori, that was Mr. Lever on the phone. He says your project is three days late and he's worried you'll get a failing grade. What's going on here and how can I help?"

Breaking the addiction to fear as a motivator can be traumatic. In the beginning you may feel that you are sending the wrong message, that you are approving their lack of performance.

Don't let that understandably anxious feeling start you back on the path of threats and intimidation. Replace the urge to spout gloom and doom with a genuine offer of help. Practice the advice in this book every time you want to berate your young person, and you won't fall back into old habits.

React Strategically to Bad News

Rationale: Bad news is never welcome, yet it always arrives bearing a gift. That gift is the opportunity to reinforce the support and love you have for your young person.

There is more goodwill to be won in the first few minutes after your kid gives you bad news than in hours of working on the relationship in other ways.

Your reaction to bad news is a litmus test for your status as a Learning Ally. Your young person is observing you. They want to know if you are really going to "walk all the talk" about helping them, or are just blowing steam. Often they are prepared to see you as a hypocrite. This is your chance to show them that you are more interested in improving performance than you are in punishing them. You can demonstrate this by reacting only to the situation, setting aside your emotional judgment of what's going on.

In response, your young person will be eternally grateful. OK, they'll be grateful for a couple of hours, anyway. And better yet, they'll be free to do the things that make this bad news less likely to be delivered again.

Reacting strategically to bad news means that you are focused on identifying the problem and causes, while suspending judgment about the situation. Reacting strategically means fixing the problem and not the blame.

How To Do It:

1. Weed out and suspend emotional reactions to the bad news that further label it as "bad."

Reacting strategically doesn't mean you have no feelings about the matter, that you aren't thoroughly, emotionally involved in the news. In no way does reacting in this fashion require you to deny your feelings. On the contrary, you have every right to your own emotional reactions, including anger, disappointment, and betrayal. It does mean, however, that you do some compartmentalizing of your thoughts. Being strategic in your reactions allows you to pick what responses are most helpful to the situation and suspend or hold off on those that probably wouldn't be productive. Usually these nonproductive responses involve judgments of the situation: good/bad, smart/stupid, thoughtful/rude.

Find more appropriate times and places to vent these reactions. It's a mental game that you play. You set your anger, disappointment, and shame aside for the moment. You tell yourself there will be lots of time later to express these emotions. Don't deny yourself. Go ahead and express them, but do it later, in a more appropriate situation, possibly with a spouse or friend. Get it out! Spew all your venom and anger! Just don't dump all this garbage on your young learner. They don't need it. What they need is your help.

2. With your knee-jerk responses on hold, you free yourself to choose from a whole smorgasbord of effective, constructive reactions that don't alienate your kid, and are much more likely to produce the kind of result you both want.

Strategic reactions have two parts:

▲ A nonjudgmental emotional response (or paraphrase)
▲ A question designed to gather more data

Strategic reactions most often begin with a genuine expression of emotion or paraphrase, then rapidly follow with a question designed to get more information.

A strategic reaction to your young person flunking chemistry might go something like this:

"Oh no! Flunking chemistry? How did this happen? You've been working so hard on it."

Notice how this seemingly inane response sends the message that you are concerned, and rapidly gets the student talking again. Remember, it's more important what ***they*** say than what ***you*** say. Get them talking as soon as possible.

Your young person might respond with, "I know, Dad, but Mr. Beeker wouldn't let me make up those missed assignments from the beginning of the semester and now I don't have enough points to pass. Do you think you could talk to him?"

Other examples of strategic reactions are:

Bad News: "I forgot to study for my math test tomorrow."

Strategic Reaction: *"You forgot to study? That's gonna make it pretty tough to do your best." (This is all the emotional response you get to express before you start to help.)*

"Let's see, how much do you think you remember? Maybe we have enough time to get you through this thing."

Bad News: "I got caught cheating on my biology quiz and received a zero."

Strategic Reaction: *"Argh! Darrel, cheating is such a bad rap. Is it true? Were you really doing what they said you were?"*

Bad News: "I haven't gone to gym class for two months!"

Strategic Reaction: *"You haven't been going to gym? You must feel pretty strongly about something going on in there. Want to tell me about it? Maybe I could help?"*

Bad News: "School no longer has any validity for me. I'm gonna quit and join a rock band!"

Strategic Reaction: *"You're going to give up your education for a life in music, huh? Sounds like you've put some thought behind this. Tell me about your decision."*

Pitfalls: **Don't panic!** Just because you don't immediately disapprove of inappropriate behavior doesn't mean you condone it. It just means you are trying to get all the data before you commit to a reaction. Later you can express your emotional responses when you've calmed down and can do it in a clear and precise manner.

Never use sarcasm! It's the least strategic of all responses. It makes you feel powerful and vindicated for a few moments, but pays negative dividends between the two of you for long afterward.

In the final analysis, it's the young person's reaction to bad news that really counts. It's how **they** address the situation that determines whether they learn and profit, or wander off on the path to more of the same. The support you give them can make all the difference.

Give Your Kid Lots of Opportunities to Fail

Rationale: Kids who have a high tolerance for failure are much more likely to succeed. They manage the ill effects of continually falling short of the mark, and consequently learn that failure is something you *do,* not something you *are.*

These young people see themselves as acting upon the world. They are happier and more productive than youngsters who perceive themselves as being acted upon.

Having a mind-set that explains success in terms of what you do rather than what is done to you is an incredible advantage. It prevents the young person from becoming a victim who's at the mercy of others. It allows them to take responsibility for their behavior and to learn from their mistakes.

Young people who see themselves whipped and lashed by the winds of chance fail to make the connection between their own personal power and achieving their goals. Their response is to whine and make excuses because they generally distrust the world and the role they play in it.

"Why bother," they say. "The odds are stacked against me, and if I do manage to get a few hits, someone will change the rules."

It's all too easy for kids to fall into this trap. The world is increasingly unfair to young people. The rules seem to change daily, even hourly. It takes a lot of energy to even keep up. Many don't. They check out and start making rules of their own. These rules are often in conflict with their needs and the norms of society.

On the other hand, there are kids who just seem to keep on plugging. Against all odds they persevere and find the pluck required to make their mark on the world. No challenge is too great and no system is so mysterious that they can't learn a few plays to run against it. They endure and smile and seem to find reward in the struggle itself.

These kids have a bias for action. They don't see the world ganging up on them. They see opportunities. They see bulls-eyes everywhere. Their only dilemma is which one to aim for first! If they miss here and there, they aren't defeated. They intuitively sense that ammunition is limitless and there are always more targets.

The ability to think and behave this way often appears to be god-given or innate. It's not! It's a learned behavior and it can be taught by you.

"There is much to be said for failure. It is more interesting than success."

Max Beerbohm

67

How To Do It:

1. Expose your young person to activities that give them lots of opportunities to "mess up" yet survive. Even better if they can mess up and survive around others who are doing the same.

Allow them to experience failure on a continuing basis in some aspect of their lives. This may be any challenging activity such as learning a musical instrument or technical skill, participating in sports, or identifying wildlife. The only requirement is that they achieve success by the continued refinement of skills that initially produce failure.

2. Invite your kid to join you in some new endeavor where you both are novices. Your example can be the greatest form of permission that they need. Side by side, you two can learn to manage the downside of never placing in a bicycle race or hitting the wrong notes on your keyboards. Your ultimate goal is to desensitize them to the occasionally destructive reactions they have to "blowing it."

Instill in them, through your good example, that failure is just the prelude to another try. Failure is fodder for ultimate success. Help them learn that great success and achievement are the result of the learning acquired from successive flubs, flops, and goofs.

3. Help your kid see that losers aren't people who fail to succeed, they're people who don't succeed at managing failure.

At an appropriate time and without preaching, point out that there are many people who don't let failures stop them. Show them examples you've clipped and saved from the news. Share anecdotes about people in your own family. Make sure they are aware of historical figures who've experienced failure, like Marie Curie, Babe Ruth, and Thomas Edison.

Pitfalls: Don't confuse helping your youngster experience failure with turning them into one.

Kids who've never learned to struggle are handicapped. Making it too easy on your child deprives them of learning to "hang in there." Don't let your chagrin at the long faces and frustration stop you from helping them acquire this crucial skill.

This is especially true if things come easy for your youngster. If they have usually accomplished everything they put their mind to, they're at risk of missing out, because no challenge has ever really taxed them. They've never really committed themselves to achieving a goal they weren't convinced was in their power.

Everyone needs that experience. Everyone needs to learn to struggle, to value the journey more than the destination. Don't let your young person miss out just because you're afraid their self-image will suffer. It will, a bit, but that's what you're there for.

Pick them up. Dust them off and send them right back into the fray.

Take Charge

By Keeping Those Doors
of Communication Open

You can't do the schoolwork for them!

It would be a lot simpler and easier, but it's not an option. All you can do, as a Learning Ally, is communicate. You share your impressions of the work that has been done or the work that should be done, or even what you did in similar circumstances, hoping they'll listen and profit from your experience. And they will, if you have the patience to give them the first shot and the courage to reciprocate with the real thing.

Create Opportunities to Listen to Your Youngster

Rationale: Mike Royko, a columnist for the Chicago *Sun-Times*, once said the best way to start a conversation with an untalkative youngster was to ask him to describe the meanest, rottenest kid in school. My tests of this technique haven't proven him wrong yet. Every kid I've asked, has had a tale to tell about the injustices and violence they've suffered at the hands of various bullies and evil-doers.

Whether you are a preschooler or a postdoctorate student, everyone has a story they need to tell. The fortunate among us have a sympathetic ear with whom we can share it. We don't expect the listener to solve our problems, approve of our behavior, or react in any particular fashion. We just appreciate their listening to us.

"The reason we have two ears and one mouth is that we may listen the more and talk the less."

Zeno of Citium

When your youngster tells a story, it helps them think through their own predicaments and come up with their own solutions. By listening to them you validate the importance of their experience. Someone has taken the time to sit down and give them their undivided attention. In doing so you earn your kid's gratitude and confidence.

Listening to your kid's stories is a classic win-win situation. You gain their respect and trust without having to solve their problems for them. The youngster gets time and a secure environment that allows them to work through dilemmas and generate their own solutions.

How To Do It:

1. Eat meals together.

The best way to create an opportunity for listening is to eat meals together. Sitting down and sharing a meal in the absence of distractions is the world's most powerful catalyst for good conversation. Sooner or later, if you eat enough meals together, your youngster will tell you what they need to get off their chests. When you make a habit of eating in this fashion, you'll be creating a readymade forum for problem-solving and trust-building to occur every morning and evening, maybe even lunchtimes.

The best possible situation is a meal at home without the interference of televisions, radios, or stereos. The Learning Ally and their young student are best seated comfortably at a table, occupying themselves with only two things, eating and conversing.

2. Capture opportunities to listen.

As a teacher I was taught that there are opportunities for learning that occur spontaneously. They happen as a result of a random event or comment that has little to do with the subject at hand, but may be rich in significance for another area of the curriculum. It was a smart instructor who stopped everything and used this windfall to teach their kids a colorful and thought-provoking lesson. We called these opportunities "teachable moments" and I, especially, was on the lookout for them. A funny thing happened, though. It seemed the more I looked for these "teachable moments," the more they happened. Pretty soon they were happening on a daily basis and I was changing my whole pattern of instruction, knowing that these serendipitous moments would appear. My class became a little more chaotic, but a lot more interesting.

Just as there are "teachable moments," there are also "listenable moments." They spontaneously happen all the time, if you look out for them. And just like my experience in the classroom, the more you are on the lookout, the more they'll occur.

"The voice is the second face."

Gerard Bauer

Assume that your young person is trying to communicate with you all the time. Be especially tuned in to their offhand comments, humor, or sarcasm. These are often forays into conversations they find uncomfortable. You'll discover there are many chances every day to listen to your kid.

Pitfalls: Listening to your young person's stories can be a wonderful experience. It's fun to share in their life and help them solve problems. It can also be a very unpleasant, gut-wrenching experience. Kids often say things you don't want to hear. Their opinions can make you mad and raise your blood pressure. Sometimes they have to deliver bad news. Don't shy away! If you want your young person to be open and honest, you must be willing to listen attentively and sympathetically to all their messages, not just the ones that make you proud or entertain you. This is a fundamental test. If you are willing to listen to all they have to say, you'll pass and the communication will flow. If you are selective, you'll fail. Communication will slow to a trickle and finally cease.

Tell Them Your Stories

Rationale: For most of human history, the lessons and customs of a society were passed by word of mouth. The essence of what it was to be a man or woman was contained in legends and stories told around campfires in communal huts. Every syllable was eagerly consumed by wide-eyed youngsters who often knew the tale by heart, yet never tired of hearing it. By young adulthood most people could tell the stories and myths of their culture to their own children.

These stories weren't just random accounts of experience. They were mythical tales of heroes and heroines who took long journeys, faced incredible dangers, overcame great obstacles, and eventually returned home. They were parables of how a person becomes an adult, how they take on the responsibility and challenges of full membership in the society. All the elements of great literature are present in these fables. They may have been tragic, humorous, mysterious, and profound, but always they were instructive.

(Instinctively, kids are enthralled by a story well-told.)

They respect and admire the people who tell them. In a very natural way they open themselves and trust the wisdom of the storyteller. In today's world, though, this can be dangerous. Kids are overwhelmed by stories from every source. They've lost the ability to be enthralled, due to the sheer volume of information. Since few of us live in a small tribal society, there isn't common agreement on the myths that describe "our" condition. Kids don't know who to pay attention to and they don't know what stories are relevant. That leaves them prey to people who would tell fables that teach how to be good little consumers or unquestioning voters.

Enthrall your youngster with the right stories, the wholesome, relevant stories, by choosing and telling them yourself. Be their storyteller and share the significant tales of your own life and the lives of good people you've known.

How To Do It: Telling a good story is like telling a good joke. You have to "wanna tell it." Your mind needs to be in the right place, or anything you say will lack power and sincerity. Getting yourself in this confident, self-assured place is easier than it may seem.

1. Select the right stories.

Share stories that have significance to you, not ones you think will have an impact on your kid. The power of your storytelling comes from within you. It's a function of your belief in the story's value and message. Your story has an impact when it's obvious you are enthusiastic and joyful (or sad) in the act of retelling it. You'll know you have a good one when you find yourself reliving the experience as it's told. You will be confident in the belief that they are darn lucky to be hearing this from you.

2. Get your story straight.

There's a beginning, middle, and end to every yarn ever spun. Make sure yours has all three as well. Take a little time beforehand to check your facts, data, and sequence of events. No matter how profound or dramatic, a good story won't just spill off your lips. It often requires a little rehearsal in front of a mirror or into a tape recorder to get that flow and logical sequence so important to credibility. Take the time needed to do justice to the experience you are sharing.

3. Tell it straight.

That is, tell it like a true storyteller does. Don't preach, don't try to convince them of anything, don't attempt to change their minds, just tell them your story and savor the experience. Story-tellers are so sure of the value of their words, they never worry about their audience. They revel in the retelling of events that had significance to them. The best actually relive these events, and by doing so honor and instruct those who would listen. In the end it's more important what you feel than what you say. A tear or a belly-laugh or a howl at the moon makes all the difference.

Pitfalls: Don't underestimate yourself. Your own life experience is the richest source of tales that will be meaningful to your youngster. Others may have had more adventures or more dramatic lives, yet you will tell your own tales with the most enthusiasm and sincerity. Include the experience of others only when you have no remotely comparable events to share.

Encourage Them to Write on a Regular Basis

Rationale: In school students learn to write. They also learn to enjoy it or hate it. By the time most kids get to 11th grade, only 39% report that they like to write!

Obviously, those who enjoy writing are at a great advantage. They find it easier and more enjoyable to learn the techniques of communicating via the written word. They develop writing skills more rapidly than other students and they use this ability to super-charge their learning in every other aspect of their education.

"A poem, a sentence, cause us to see ourselves. I be, and I see my being at the same time."

Ralph Waldo Emerson

Students learn to be good writers by getting a lot of practice. It doesn't matter whether they write letters to their grandmother or to sports heroes or pen-pals. It's the activity that's important. Transferring their thoughts into words on paper develops a relationship between your student and that blank page. Instead of a fearful, agonizing challenge that a composition often represents, the student who regularly writes sees an open canvas, an inviting outlet for ideas, feelings, and concerns, a vehicle with which they can act upon the world. Writing makes young people powerful and confident.

How To Do It:

1. Encourage your kid to keep a journal.

Ideally a student should write every day. Whether it's a little or a lot, they should write every day in a composition notebook or journal. This collection of their thoughts is strictly their own personal business. They alone determine who they show it to. This daily writing should not be directed. It should be writing for writing's sake. This free form of writing generates the raw material for the more polished stories, reports, and letters that come later.

Encourage your young person to spend at least fifteen uninterrupted minutes a day adding material to this journal.

They should spend an additional five to ten minutes reviewing what they have written on previous days. Offer to read and critique anything they might be willing to share with you, but make sure that you encourage and reinforce the volume of their work, not necessarily the quality. Remember, it's practice that develops the writer.

2. Help them use the four-step method.

In more formal writing assignments (but <u>not</u> in their journal), help your young person use the four-step process of **brainstorming, composing, revising,** and **editing** to produce writing that expresses what they want to say, and does so interestingly.

▲ **Brainstorm:** Think, discuss, research, draw, diagram, doodle, build a model, or write in stream-of-consciousness mode so as to generate the raw material for a creative piece of writing. Make a mess. Don't worry about form, spelling topic, or grammar. Just let your mind travel where it wants, but make sure you document these travels in some fashion.

▲ **Compose:** Write a first draft as fast as you can. It might be full of mistakes and poor word choices but keep going. String the sentences together and get a feel for the tone and rhythm of the piece. Speak the words to yourself as you compose. Dramatize the inflection and imagine yourself saying these things as you write them down. Remember, you're building a "straw horse" at this point. There will be a lot of opportunity for fine-tuning later.

▲ **Revise:** Look at what you've got. Do more research on new areas that have cropped up. Show it to some people. Ask the hard questions like, "Does this make any sense?" Then fix up the parts that don't work and put things in the right order (the sequence of your ideas often changes as much as the words you use to describe them).

▲ **Edit:** Set your work aside for a period of time (two days . . . two hours?) Give yourself some distance from the work. Then fanatically check for details large and small. Build the power and persuasiveness of the piece through attention to the details of proper spelling, grammar, and usage.

3. Write yourself.

Once again, you are the single, most powerful influence. If you want them to write, let them see *you* doing it. On a regular basis, make a spectacle of yourself enjoying the act of writing. It really is infectious. Invite your youngster to join you. Compose twin letters to Grandma and seal them in the same envelope. Write alternating lines of the same poem, or just sit together and write in your personal journals. Make it clear this is a skill that's good for you as well as them.

Pitfalls: Don't forget to let your kid get crazy. Unless you allow this to happen, your student will never connect their wild creative side with the side that makes sense of it all.

Young people won't write unless they have a reason. The reason must be theirs, not yours. Don't let them give up. There are many valid reasons for them to write, not the least of which is, it makes you, their Learning Ally, happy.

Make sure they have the proper tools. Interesting stationery and a good writing implement always help. Stimulate their literary impulses with creative reasons to put pen to paper. You might find yourself carrying on a dialog through the exchange of daily journals you both keep. What a great way to keep the lines of communication open!

Read to Your Young Person

Rationale: Young people who are read to by the adults in their life become better readers. They have superior skill in the actual process of reading, as well as improved motivation and enthusiasm for reading on their own.

"Some books are to be tasted, others to be swallowed, and some few to be chewed and digested."

Francis Bacon

83

Some adults go even further, literally tutoring their kids with workbooks and other instructional aids. However, this approach doesn't seem to produce significant performance improvements. Kids who sit down with an adult and have a story read to them on a regular basis do just as well. The bottom line is: the more experiences your youngster has with reading, the better.

 **How To Do It:** This is probably the most simple thing to do in this whole book. Set aside some time, sit down with the kid in your life, and read to them. Don't worry if they are too young or too old. Everyone from preschoolers to high school students profit from this activity. The Learning Ally's job is to have confidence in this knowledge and share the joy of reading.

Choose to read a story you love. Don't agonize over what your youngster will enjoy. If the reading selection "lives" for you, if it's profoundly affected your life, they'll enjoy it, too, and you'll do a better job of reading.

If they do have preferences, go ahead and read them. It's OK to read their favorites over and over again, as this kind of repetition is instructive in itself. Don't, however, forget **your** stories, because part of your goal in reading to them is to expose your youngster to new and varied forms of literature. Mix it up. Include poetry, drama, nonfiction—whatever you find intriguing.

When you read to a young person, "the end" does not mean the experience is finished. "The end" means the beginning of a dialog about what went on in the story. Ask your kid some probing questions about the material. Go beyond the surface of names and places. Really pry into their minds by asking questions about motivation, emotion, plot, and character.

You might ask questions like these:

"Why do you think Eric did such a foolish thing?"

"What do you think the author's position is on logging in the national park? Why?"

"How would you end this story? Would you do anything different? Why?"

"If you were Alexis, would you have fought? Why?"

"When you hear poems like this, what kind of images do you see?"

"Tell me why it's a good/bad story."

In the answers to these questions is the conversation that will make your reading time even more valuable. Kids learn that reading is more than just decoding a bunch of words. They learn it's a springboard to intellectual activity. Whether you read them a fiery poem or a detailed scientific treatise, kids will soon see that "the end" is just the beginning!

Pitfalls: Don't let the fact that you aren't the most eloquent reader in the world keep you from this activity. You don't need to be. You don't even need to be a good reader. Your kid doesn't care if you can't decipher every word right away. They don't care if you have to start over once in a while. They care that **you** care enough to sit down and read them a story you love.

Take Charge

By Setting the Stage
For Success

At best, a Learning Ally can only be a stagehand for the great performances youngsters put on at school.

When the big moment comes, when the music reaches a crescendo and the spotlight bathes your kid, you'll be in the wings confidently enjoying the show. Your optimism comes from the knowledge that you've created an environment that supports their best work. This chapter outlines steps you can take to insure the quality of your kid's personal environment (their health), and the physical surroundings of their study area.

Help Your Kid Stay Physically Fit

Rationale: A sound body is the best foundation for a mind that is ready and able to learn. Your youngster will only do their best mental work when they are in top physical shape. Some problems with learning have their roots in readily identifiable health problems. Making sure your student maintains a level of physical fitness that supports their best work is a good way to rule out these health-based problems, and it compliments all the efforts you make as their Learning Ally.

It's a mistake to assume that your kid's youth guarantees good physical condition. In fact, you're better off assuming just the opposite. Kids are less active today, they watch more TV, eat more junk food, and in general have less access to medical care than your generation.

"All the soarings of my mind begin in my blood."

Rainer Maria Rilke

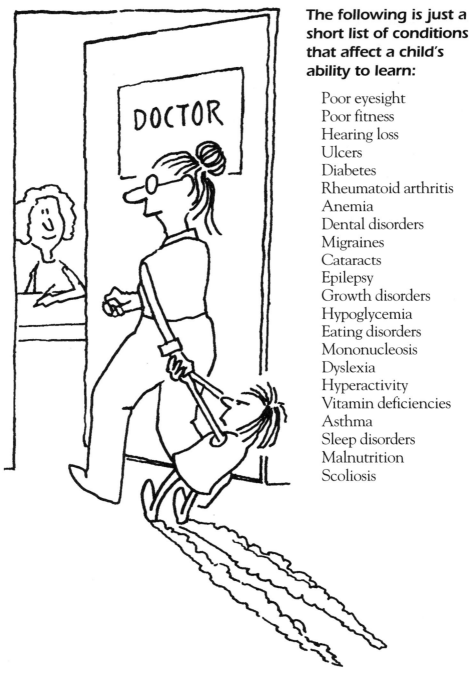

The following is just a short list of conditions that affect a child's ability to learn:

Poor eyesight
Poor fitness
Hearing loss
Ulcers
Diabetes
Rheumatoid arthritis
Anemia
Dental disorders
Migraines
Cataracts
Epilepsy
Growth disorders
Hypoglycemia
Eating disorders
Mononucleosis
Dyslexia
Hyperactivity
Vitamin deficiencies
Asthma
Sleep disorders
Malnutrition
Scoliosis

How To Do It:

1. Schedule a regular physical exam for your kid.

Build a good foundation of health by making sure your young person gets a complete physical checkup at least once a year. Recognize that no one enjoys this process, so you might have to combine the visit to the clinic with something pleasant like a movie or an outing of their choice. Do this every August or September without fail, so that soon you've established a habit. Physical examinations should become just another thing that happens in the fall, like shopping for school supplies or new shoes.

If you have specific concerns about your youngster, talk to the doctor first. Be as precise as you can about the kind of difficulties your young person is experiencing. Describe what impact the disorder seems to be having on their studies, and don't worry about how far-fetched it may sound. Your hunches and feelings are a great resource to a savvy physician.

If you're like most busy adults, it's probably time you had an exam as well. Be a good role model and take some of your own medicine. Get that funny-looking mole checked out or have your cholesterol tested. Show your youngster that you know how valuable a healthy body is to a healthy mind.

2. Take responsibility for your kid's nutritional needs.

Young people need to eat at least three balanced meals a day. The most important of these meals is ***breakfast.*** If your kid is skipping this meal, they can't possibly be doing their best. All children profit from starting the day with an unhurried, warm breakfast that's consumed at the table in a seated position. It's especially helpful if there are others present to share the meal and conversation. If there is no time to do this in your schedule, you are too busy. Rearrange the morning's agenda so you can eat together. Get up a half-hour earlier if you have to. You'll be amazed at the immediate rewards to everyone when the day is started properly.

Lunch is a simpler proposition. Most schools serve a hot meal at midday, and usually it is nutritious, if not the most tasty fare around. With financial assistance to most low-income children, there is little reason for not getting a good midday meal. Better yet, help your youngster learn to make and pack their own nutritious meal for lunchtime. This promotes responsibility and gives them practice in planning and preparing actual meals.

The evening meal presents several challenges, as it precedes the most sedentary part of the day. Calories need to be high enough to satisfy hunger yet low enough to be burned. Kids are often famished at this time of day, so it's especially difficult not to start habits of snacking or overeating. Again, getting them involved in the preparation is an effective ploy. It keeps them busily occupied in

cooking rather than ravenously lying around waiting for the meal to be served. Dinner, like all meals, is best eaten seated at a table with the rest of the family. The television and radio should be turned off while the family eats and shares the experiences of their day.

Some kids burn calories at a phenomenal rate and will require snacks in between their normal meals. Fruits, grains, and vegetables are the best snacks—they meet a kid's cravings while providing lots of nutrition and fiber.

3. Encourage regular exercise.

Normal physical education requirements fall far short of the amount of exercise your youngster needs to be fit. Taking PE in school is not enough. Most kids need additional strenuous activity on a daily basis to build proper muscle and stamina. Help them and help yourself by participating in an exercise program together. Find a mutually acceptable activity like jogging or swimming, and support each other in meeting your personal physical and aerobic requirements. This is an especially valuable partnership because the kid's skills often surpass those of their Learning Ally. Take the opportunity to let them lead!

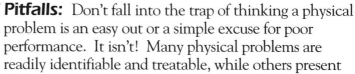

Pitfalls: Don't fall into the trap of thinking a physical problem is an easy out or a simple excuse for poor performance. It isn't! Many physical problems are readily identifiable and treatable, while others present significant challenges to a child's development. Difficulties based in a young person's habits and attitudes are much more amenable to your efforts. Here, at least, you have some flexibility in coming up with a remedy. Solutions can be found at home, and you, the Learning Ally, can be part of them.

Remember, a physical checkup is just that—a fairly general checkup done by your regular family doctor. It should not be confused with the much more involved and complex procedure of testing and evaluation that would accompany the suspicion of a learning disability such as dyslexia. In this yearly physical exam you just want to make sure all the youngster's parts are working OK and their general level of health supports high achievement. Habits of nutrition and exercise are learned at home, often before a child even starts school. That doesn't mean bad habits can't be unlearned, but a good role model is the best teacher. Take every opportunity to demonstrate your support for these wholesome approaches to personal health. If you do fall off the wagon, try to do it far from your impressionable youngster.

Create a Study Stadium In Your Home

Rationale: Anyone who has ever played sandlot baseball knows the awesome feeling of finally getting the chance to play in a genuine stadium. The environment tells you that this is serious business! Everything is set up for the needs of a genuine baseball player. The playing surface is level and smooth. The grass is emerald green and the dirt so fine, you could slide all day and never get a scratch. The whole environment seems to say, "Here's a place to do your best."

"A place for everything, everything in its place."

Benjamin Franklin

Help your kid create a "study stadium" that sends the same serious message. Build a work environment for them that supports their very best efforts and provides the tools that make success easy. Build a place for study that is a physical representation of your commitment to their achievement.

Young people are naturally drawn to places like this. They want to be involved in serious work. So give them a serious place to do it. Their minds will literally shift gears upon entering it. They'll find it easy to get into the "study mode" and to make use of all the tools that are readily at hand.

 **How To Do It:** A study stadium doesn't require a rosewood desk, super-fast computer, and the latest reference library. In fact, much of the furniture and many of the resource books can be gleaned from secondhand shops, garage sales, and the basements of family and friends. The emphasis should be on function, not flash. Build a corner of the world that belongs to your young person—a place that is singularly focused on their access to knowledge.

A study stadium should be quiet and private. It should be an environment where there are few distractions, away from the sights and sounds of television, radio, and other people. Your young person needs to be surrounded by firm reminders that their learning is a high priority. Whether you find this place in a corner of a bedroom, the basement, or even the garage is not important. What is important is the message it sends your kid, and that message is "Here's a place to do your best work!"

The study stadium should have:

Desk or table at proper height
Comfortable straight-back chair
Strong gooseneck or adjustable lamp
Pens, pencils, felt tips, crayons
Desk encyclopedia
Filing cabinet, box, or drawer
Correction fluid
Pencil sharpener
Ruler
Tape, glue, paste
Stapler
Hole punch
Paper (writing/construction)
Paper clips
Posters/photos
Rubber bands

Dictionary
Almanac
Thesaurus
Atlas
Highlight pens
Erasers
Paints
Bookshelves
Bulletin board
Protractor
Calculator
Compass
Alarm clock
Globe (blow-up?)
Scissors
Wastebasket

Don't worry if your child is too young to use some of these items. It's good that they become familiar with the tools of education. Who knows how much learning results from fooling around with things we aren't formally prepared to use?

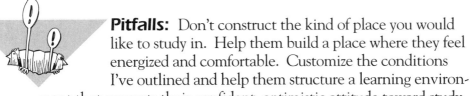

Pitfalls: Don't construct the kind of place you would like to study in. Help them build a place where they feel energized and comfortable. Customize the conditions I've outlined and help them structure a learning environment that supports their confident, optimistic attitude toward study.

The study stadium should be a safe environment where your kid spends time learning. It's best if that is the only use to which this area is put. It shouldn't be the same place they watch TV, store junk, or hang out with their friends. A study stadium has the singular purpose of supporting your kid's best work. Don't send mixed signals by adding other functions.

Fill Their Environment with Books

Rationale: Research shows that kids who spend considerable time reading for leisure do better in school than kids who spend a comparable amount of time watching TV or playing video games. Excessive time in front of the television is directly associated with poor performance in school. When your kid increases the time spent reading for pleasure their vocabulary improves, their comprehension is deeper,

"What is a book? Everything and nothing. The eye that sees it is all."

Ralph Waldo Emerson

and they become more fluent readers. You can help by creating a rich environment of reading material that makes it more likely your youngster will choose to read rather than watch TV.

How To Do It: Surround your youngster with lots of books. Make sure the books come from every conceivable subject area and format. Include everything from classics to pop-up picture books. Pay special attention to topics and categories that are new.

Help your young person create their own one-hundred-book library. Start with the books they already have, then set a goal of attaining a one-hundred-book collection in the next thirty days. In some cases this means you must get fifty books in a few weeks. In others the challenge is greater. You may be looking for the whole one hundred. Don't be overwhelmed. Finding one hundred good books is easier and cheaper than you think.

Begin your search at the local thriftshop. Books in these stores usually run from a couple of pennies to a couple of bucks. Take your kid with you and start grazing through the stacks. Rapidly select books that you think they might read, while your youngster plods through looking for just the right thing. Take the shotgun approach

and grab anything you think will entertain them. Don't worry if you pick out a few losers. Think of yourself as a pearl diver collecting lots of oysters in order to harvest a few pearls. In the end, only a small percentage of the books either of you select will be read cover to cover. The rest will be picked up once or twice, maybe skimmed or partially read, yet still they'll have been of value.

Another place to get books cheap is at garage sales. In fact, you can often get them free, especially if you go around on Sunday afternoon. By this time people are anxious to part with as much stuff as possible. Feel no guilt. Greedily take all the books they have and sort through them later.

Relatives and friends are often happy to make some space in their own homes by parting with their grown kids' dusty old reading collections. Don't worry if these books appear to be out of date. Take them anyway. Your youngster often isn't as discriminating as you might think, and it's hard to predict what titles will turn them on.

All one hundred books should be placed in your young person's room, or somewhere in the house that is formally set aside as their own personal library. Make sure this place is near their usual hangouts in the home. Make it easy to grab a book if they are bored. Make it easier than grabbing the remote TV control. In fact, hide all those remote controls under a stack of books!

Pitfalls: This library may become quite messy at times, especially if it is well used. Resist the temptation to nag your youngster or to just clear the whole mess out. Try to catch them doing right. Reinforce your kid when they take responsibility for their library by keeping it neat and orderly. Buy them a brand new book or poster as a reward. In the end, tolerate a chaotic pile of books as long as it's used as a library.

Take Charge

By Scheduling Success

▲▲▲▲▲▲▲▲▲▲▲▲▲▲▲▲▲▲▲▲▲▲▲▲▲▲

In education, the winners have to be present to pick up the prize. Make sure you show up for the learning sweepstakes that take place daily. Follow the advice in this chapter and become a consistent, stable force in your kid's schooling. A fair amount of discipline and commitment will pay off in a youngster who trusts your intentions, judgment, and counsel.

Have a Conference with Your Kid Every Day

Rationale: Nothing sends the message of your support more directly than the giving of your undivided attention. Meeting with your student on a daily basis is the way to send this message. Your job in this meeting is to be a sounding board. This means that listening is the primary skill you will use.

Kids are capable of generating many of their own solutions to academic problems. What they need most is your support. In this case the support takes the form of an interested and helpful listener—an advocate. By being available every day, you help them stay on track.

"Not only to say the right thing in the right place, but far more difficult, to leave unsaid the wrong thing at the tempting moment."

Georgé Sala

Your goal during this daily conference is to give them the opportunity to talk about how things are going, not to generate solutions to all their problems. Think of it as a chance to reduce the number of crises you'll have to deal with. By conferencing, you talk a little on a daily basis to avoid having to talk a lot in a pressure situation.

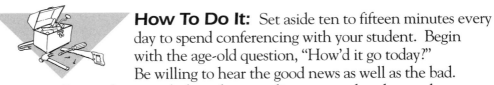

How To Do It: Set aside ten to fifteen minutes every day to spend conferencing with your student. Begin with the age-old question, "How'd it go today?" Be willing to hear the good news as well as the bad. Remember, your kid needs you to listen more than he needs you to agree or understand. The power of this tool is in your ability to receive the information they have to give.

You are listening for two kinds of information: things that are going right and things that are going wrong.

It's critical that you get information about both, because you are modeling and reinforcing this process. You want your student to make a habit of constantly appraising their own performance in order to expand upon the things that are working and find alternatives to the things that aren't.

1. Ask about the positives.

Focus first on the positives. It allows the student to build on their successes. Starting with successes also gives you an opportunity to give them praise and approval. You might say something like, *"OK, Glenda, how'd it go today? What did you like about your day?"* Or in a more lighthearted fashion, *"Glenda, tell me of your triumphs today. What mountains did you climb? What ramparts did you storm?"*

Don't accept no for an answer. Something goes well every day, if only the fact that they arrived at school in one piece. It's important to help them identify this information, as it builds the habit of looking for the positives, even when they're well hidden. Once you've heard about what's going well, compliment them or give them praise. Kids often don't see the pivotal role they have in making things go right. Point these things out to them. Help them recognize their own contributions to success.

2. Ask about the negatives.

Once you've explored the positive side, ask them where they are experiencing difficulty. You might say,

"All right, Lupe, you've got a pretty good handle on math and your science project. Did anything happen today that has you concerned?"

Again, don't take no for an answer. There's always something that goes wrong, even if it's "no big deal."

Every kid experiences failures, even if they do well in school. Awkward moments, unplanned events, out-and-out flops can all be discussed, analyzed, and ultimately prevented from becoming major hassles. Be sure to listen to this data with the same intensity as you did the positive, even though it's a lot harder to hear. Don't get too detailed at this point. Don't jump to solutions. Just listen and allow them to vent their frustrations about schoolwork, teachers, students, and life in general. Then be there to help them construct solutions of their own.

3. Review returned work.

Once you've discussed the positive and negatives of the day, you can review the work they've got back. Be sure to look at every piece of work. Students won't value returned work assignments if you don't. Help them see this material as a resource, a springboard to achievement, full of good things they should continue doing and also containing mistakes and problems they need to find alternatives for. Ensure that whatever they missed or continue to have questions about, is now clear to them.

4. Help your student set a reachable goal for the next day.

End the conference by helping them set a goal for the next day. Make sure that it's measurable and attainable, but most of all, make sure it's a goal that means something to your kid. This might be anything from standing up to the class bully to practicing relaxation exercises during a chemistry quiz. When you meet again, check on their performance and set a new goal. Above all, make sure the goal set is theirs and not yours.

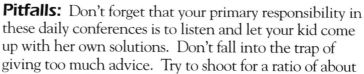

Pitfalls: Don't forget that your primary responsibility in these daily conferences is to listen and let your kid come up with her own solutions. Don't fall into the trap of giving too much advice. Try to shoot for a ratio of about 80% listening to 20% talking. If you do, your kid will have a much better chance of learning to solve her own problems.

Don't be afraid to share your own experience. It's valuable data that can be highly useful as long as you don't try to impose your own problem-solving techniques on them. You might say something like,

"Oh yeah, Dale, I had a similar situation when I was in seventh grade. My best friend always expected me to share homework answers on the bus each morning. I knew it was dishonest but didn't know how to tell her without sounding like a goody-two-shoes. What I finally did was . . . What do you think you should do?"

The great thing about sharing your own experiences is you needn't have been successful yourself to be of help to your youngster. You just need to add a little more data for them to analyze before coming up with their own solutions.

Have Your Kid Keep a Homework Log

Rationale: When your student writes down their homework assignment in a notebook, it formalizes the act of taking responsibility for their actions. Seeing those assignments, with dates and teachers' names written clearly, reinforces your young person's belief that he has control over his own success.

Showing you the information during the conference accomplishes two things. First of all, you get an opportunity to compliment them on their conscientiousness and organization, and secondly, they can take advantage of any help or guidance you might provide.

"We must ask where we are and whither we are tending."

Abraham Lincoln

Keeping a homework log and reviewing it together each night frees you both from those cat-and-mouse games over whether there is homework and if so, has it been completed? It simply becomes part of your evening's pattern to check the work to be done and collaborate on how best to do it. No more leading questions from you and no more vague answers from them—just a partnership to get their homework done in a quality fashion.

 **How To Do It:** Give your kid a small spiral-bound notebook, preferably one that can be carried in a coat or pants pocket. It's important that this book be handy and available at a moment's notice. You want the act of keeping track of responsibilities as easy and simple as possible. Show them how to divide the pages into columns and rows that leave room for the pertinent data about all assignments. This includes long-term projects as well as the smallest daily assignments. Everything that is expected of your student should be reflected in this log.

Data that should be collected on all assignments:

▲ Today's date
▲ Name of the class
▲ Name of the instructor
▲ Description of the assignment
▲ Due date
▲ Estimate of time required in minutes

 **Pitfalls:** Make sure that you both go over this log every day. Don't miss a day! The collaboration between you two is more important than actually finishing every bit of work every night. Your goal is to establish a habit, a pleasant ritual of mutually scanning the evening's work and finding a strategy to get it all done well. It should not be viewed by either of you as some kind of "inspection."

Save Everything Your Kid Produces at School

Rationale: Saving all schoolwork sends a strong message to your student. It says that their efforts are worth something. Every assignment, whether it's "A" work or not, is seen as a valuable piece of the puzzle. Solving the puzzle of high achievement will require students to look hard at all the pieces, not just their best work. Too often, good work is all you ever see. The assignments that show your youngster needs help in math or reading often end up swirling in the wind somewhere between school and home.

"We can chart our future clearly and wisely only when we know the path which has led to the present."

Adlai Stevenson

When you review and save all work, you show your kid that everything is important. That miserable math assignment can prove to be valuable in helping avoid the same mistakes in the future. Saving it can set them up for success, just as saving fine work helps youngsters take pride in their achievement and see what they must continue doing.

Treat all work as valuable and your kid can break the habit of broadcasting good assignments and hiding or destroying their poor work. They'll understand it's a losing game to cut themselves off from critical data that will help them excel. They'll soon see that these papers form an ongoing record of their progress as well as a ready supply of review material for use in preparing for tests.

Keeping all of your student's work also gives you a wealth of material to use in contacts with teachers and administrators. Often parents are confronted at conference time with a mass of grades in a book. With nothing to back up their impressions, they must rely on the teacher's information, which is fine until there's a disagreement. Having your own data, in the form of daily work, can be a great resource. After all, it's the raw material from which all conclusions about your kid's progress are made. If you've saved it, you can come with an armful of material to support your conclusions.

 **How To Do It:** Get a cardboard box and put all of your student's finished work in it. The box should be at least 2x3 feet and a foot deep. You can get as tricky with the organization as you wish. Make separate files for each course area, or time, and date everything. Do whatever makes you both comfortable and allows access to the data on your student's progress.

Remember to save *everything!* That includes school flyers, notes home, progress reports, and work your kid discards without turning it in. Everything is fair game for "the box" except, of course, the work you display on the refrigerator, and that, too, goes into the box when it finally turns brown and curly from age.

At the end of each year or term, you and your student can go through the box and decide what materials and projects are worth saving for posterity, and what stuff goes to the recycle bin. Then start the process all over again.

Pitfalls: Remember, everything is important. Look at everything your kid does and make a mark and date that indicates you've done so. Your purpose is to build a file of materials that can substantiate accurate judgments about how your student is doing. Some work is more important than the rest and will get a lot of your attention. Other work will be glanced at and just filed.

Evaluate Progress Monthly

Rationale: Frequent self-evaluation is a powerful tool in helping a student monitor achievement. Often kids lose track of their progress in the middle of a term and miss opportunities for those all-important, mid-course corrections. They don't see their activities globally. They see the present quite clearly while yesterday, tomorrow, and beyond are pretty fuzzy. They need your help because they often won't evaluate their performance until it's too late.

A habit of routine, constructive self-evaluation will serve your young person well in the future. Most kids spend an inordinate amount of time ruminating over how poorly they stack up against other kids, adults, or heroes in their life. They're unrealistic about what they could be doing, and consequently are much harder on themselves than they should be. Monthly opportunities for specific self-evaluation let them form a more accurate and "down to earth" impression of their capabilities.

How To Do It: Get a blank copy of their report card and make several copies of it. Every four weeks spend part of your conference time filling it out with your student. Better yet, they should fill it out and you should watch. Once they've finished they can tell you about each subject area and explain any comments they've made or trends that are appearing. They should be able to back up any and all grades they give. All improvement and deterioration should be explained and substantiated.

An effective variation on this process is to have your student play the role of the teacher and give you the report card. You play the role of your kid. Make it fun! Challenge the teacher (your kid!) and make them show you data that supports the grades they're giving you. Also model appropriate responses to compliments and criticism from the teacher.

You may also want to use this monthly self-evaluation as an opportunity to reward progress toward their goals. If they think they are doing well, reward them. Take their word for it and spring for a trip to the movies or a weekend outing. The best reward is always an opportunity to have your undivided attention. (For more on rewards, see Chapter 2.)

"One cool judgment is worth a thousand hasty councils. The thing to do is supply light and not heat."

Woodrow Wilson

113

Remember, you are helping to establish a habit of self-evaluation. It's more important to get practice in doing this kind of assessment than it is to produce a perfectly accurate report card. Allow for a little fogginess or fudging on the grades to begin with. Kids become better evaluators with time, as they see how powerful it is to be proactive and honest with themselves.

Your goal is to break down the fear and complacency that many kids have about grades by giving them a chance to co-opt the system. Soon they'll be comfortable doing to themselves what formerly they were afraid the system would do to them.

Pitfalls: Self-evaluations are not to be confused with opportunities to beat up on yourself. You want to foster an attitude of constructive optimism, regardless of how unskilled your youngster may be in a particular area. Remind kids who are having difficulties that it's more important where they are heading than where they are.

Don't just file this information away. You can use the report card your kid has generated as a springboard for good discussion during the monthly meetings with their teacher (see Chapter 7). First of all check for validity. Make sure that what your youngster thinks is true is also true from the teacher's perspective. Together you can develop strategies to bring up falling marks and maintain good ones, always trying to bring your student's performance in line with the high expectations they have for themselves.

Help Them Drill

Rationale: A lot of what your youngster does in school is focused on building a data base of information that she will use in solving problems of a higher level. These problems typically require more than just immediate recall of facts. Their solutions compel her to analyze, synthesize, and otherwise manipulate the facts she has memorized. If the development of this data base is left to chance, it will be filled with gaps. She will have difficulty calling upon needed data, and all too often the data recalled will be incorrect. As a result she will experience more failure and frustration in school.

"Repetition is the mother of learning."

Russian Proverb

Kids don't know what they don't know.

They often read through material once and hope that they can remember it come test time. When they fail to retain the facts, they think it's because they are stupid or didn't study hard enough. Learning something "by heart" requires repeated exposures. It requires drill. A Learning Ally serves as a drill partner who provides repetitive practice that builds accurate, readily available data bases.

The time to determine whether your kid knows what they need to know is *before* they take the test. Students who have an adult to check their understanding through drill and review techniques have the advantage of ***knowing what they know.*** If there is material they can't recall, more drill and practice can fill in the knowledge gaps.

How To Do It:

1. Determine what your student must know.

Usually an instructor will publish a list or study sheet of the material they expect students to know "by heart." Make sure you have a copy of all these papers. If your kid has lost them or doesn't know what it is they must know, you'll need to contact the teacher. Ask them what it is that your kid needs to know by heart. Don't accept vague answers like, "Well, they need to know the material in chapter five." Insist on knowing what material in chapter five is important. In fact, it's fair to ask what material in chapter five will turn up on any tests or quizzes. After all, that's what your kid is expected to learn, isn't it? Don't accept assignments that require your kid to guess what it is they need to know. Every teacher should be able to state precisely what this material is. Every student should know what it is they are trying to learn.

2. Help your student organize the information.

This can be as simple as writing math facts or historical dates on 3x5 cards and laying them out on the floor in some logical sequence. However, the organization and display of the data should differ from the way it is presented in class. Make it bigger, more colorful, or unique in some way. Write the names of presidents on balloons or draw a giant periodic table of the elements in chalk on the patio. Tantalize them with a unique yet logical presentation that frames the data in a new and intriguing fashion.

3. Be their drill partner.

Think of yourself as an automatic pitching machine. Your sole job is to serve up perfect ball after ball. It's your student's job to take their best swing. Don't evaluate or analyze or make any judgments at all while you are drilling them. Behave in a very machinelike and matter-of-fact way. Quiz them in a manner that most simply and directly separates the known information from the unknown. Show them flash cards, ask the meaning of vocabulary terms, or simply point to random math problems on a fact sheet. Your role is to support the repetitive exposure of material, not to teach anything. This also frees you from having to understand everything you are helping them learn.

4. Keep score.

Let your kid keep track of their own performance. It's often helpful for the student to graph the results of each drill session and display the graph in their study area. This way they can see the inevitable progress made and give themselves credit. You are kept out of the evaluation business and maintain your status as a non-judgmental drill partner.

Pitfalls: Don't forget to be nonjudgmental. You aren't a cheerleader or a taskmaster. You are there to help your kid drill, and it's that practice you can feel free to praise. Don't worry about their performance within the session. The learning will come with repetition. The habit they develop of drilling and practice will be the result of your presence and approval.

Don't get stuck in a rut. Possibly the most important role you play in their drill will be a creative one. Pop those balloons with the presidents' names on them after your kid correctly identifies the year they were elected. Let them explain the periodic table to your bridge club as the card players walk among the elements. Use your experience and imagination to make normally mundane practice fun and stimulating.

Teach Your Student Memory Tricks

Rationale: Kids who can quickly and accurately recall information are perceived as intelligent and capable. They usually are. Good memories are linked with high IQ's. But does your kid need to be a genius in order to recall information well? The answer is no. Your youngster can have perfectly normal intellectual abilities, yet use memory techniques that allow them to recall data at a phenomenal level.

"Memory is the cabinet of imagination, the treasury of reason, the registry of conscience and the council chamber of thought."

Saint Basil

The payoff is twofold. First of all, your kid has greater access to the data they need to solve more complex problems. Secondly, a "halo effect" occurs, since they are perceived by their teachers as more able and in need of challenge. Your student has a greater chance of success because their higher achievement reinforces expectations held by their educators.

How To Do It: There are two memory techniques that you can teach your student:

1. Structured Review

People often fail to recognize just how often material must be reviewed in order to be retained in the long-term memory. Review is more than just repetition of the material over and over. It's more than drill. It's repetition within a plan, punctuated by checks for accuracy. Noted learning expert Tony Buzan emphasizes in his book *Make the Most of Your Mind* that it should start almost immediately after the new material has been presented and continue at a reducing rate for a period of days, weeks, and months. If the review is done with diligence the new material becomes as accessible as a phone number or address.

Proper review is the result of disciplined scheduling. Help your youngster determine the critical information they need to learn and then teach them this variation of Mr. Buzan's technique of review:

▲ The first time you are exposed to a new idea, review it immediately. Say it, write it, and say it again.

▲ Sixty minutes later, do the same thing. Say it, write it, and say it again.

▲ Before going to bed the next three nights, say it, write it, and say it again.

▲ Do the same thing, once each week, in the following three weeks.

▲ On a monthly basis, review in this fashion, until the material is easily recalled with 100% accuracy.

Use your skill as a nonjudgmental drill partner to quickly run through the words, concepts, and skills they are trying to commit to memory. ***Always shoot for 100% retention.*** "Close enough" is not good enough. If you and your student determine that something is worth remembering, it should be completely and accurately remembered. Help them start now with this habit of 100% accuracy and it will serve them well in the future.

On the other hand, don't spend time and effort memorizing material that doesn't warrant it. There is nothing more damaging to a kid's attitude than to work hard to learn material that is just regurgitated on a test and forgotten, or even worse, never asked for at all. Insist that the material your kid is required to memorize is central to the subject studied and is used as a springboard for further learning.

2. Mnemonic Devices

Most of the astounding feats of memory we see in show business are the result of memory tricks. These tricks allow people to make links in their minds between the material to be recalled and self-generated images that have personal significance.

As students most of us used a mnemonic device to remember the notes in the musical scale. We were taught the sentence "Every good boy does fine" and consequently remembered the notes were EGBDF, the first letters of each word in the sentence. Linking this easily recalled sentence with a seemingly unrelated set of letters is the magic of mnemonic devices. They connect logical or easily recalled information to new data, creating pathways from the known and familiar. This is a powerful technique because it mirrors the natural way the brain acquires information.

Mnemonic devices rely on the ability of your kid to come up with a vivid, personally significant idea and pair it with new information. These ideas usually come from topics related to their interests, hobbies, and friends, or jokes and wild notions that stem from these areas. Help them be creative, even absurd, when they are generating ideas to link with the new material. Examples of this might be:

▲ A group of their friends, each wearing an outfit that corresponds with the colors of the spectrum

▲ Starting a nonsensical sentence with the first letter of each planet in the solar system

▲ The thirteen original colonies as positions on a football team, with offensive and defensive coaches

Help your youngster come up with these connections by making suggestions that have worked or could work for you. From there help them generate their own wild and novel connections. Then commence your drill routine on the schedule discussed above.

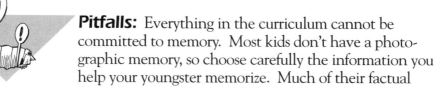

Pitfalls: Everything in the curriculum cannot be committed to memory. Most kids don't have a photographic memory, so choose carefully the information you help your youngster memorize. Much of their factual learning will be out of date by the time they reach adulthood, and it would be a shame to spend time memorizing things they need only regurgitate once on a test. Yet for some kids this process of learning is the primary way they acquire information. If that's the case with your kid, don't argue with success. Just support them in the best, most creative way you can.

Some facts, concepts, and principles pay high dividends as a result of their absolute memorization. The following is an incomplete list:

Math:
> Addition facts to twelve
> Subtraction facts to twelve
> Multiplication facts to twelve
> Division facts to twelve

English:
> Common prefixes
> Common suffixes
> Common root words
> Vowels

Geography:
> States and capitals of the USA
> Countries of the world
> Continents
> Rivers/lakes of the USA
> Rivers/bodies of water in the world

History:
> Historical periods
> Historical people
> Historical events

Memorizing something out of context is hard, which is why memory tricks build links. Explain the "why" first and the young person will find it easier to expend the effort.

Visit the Local Library at Least Once a Month

Rationale: Regarding libraries, there are two types of kids: those who see them as prisons, and those who see them as amusement parks. Kids who do well in school are the same kids who step through those library doors as if they were the gates to the wildest ride in the park.

Young people who are turned on by libraries know that they are places of infinite stimulation and challenge. They see the library as a place to solve problems, settle arguments, and start new

controversies. The library becomes an important part of their personal educational journey. In many ways it helps a young person see themselves as an individual who is independent and capable.

High technology has not made libraries obsolete. The vast majority of information your youngster needs is still found in books. This will be true for a long time to come, regardless of the leaps made in computer technology. Your kid is better off being "library literate" than "computer literate." Top-notch students know this. They know that computers, at their best, only speed up the processes that often are most logically accomplished among the stacks of a good library.

"When you read a classic, you do not see more in the book than you did before; you see more in you than there was before."

Clifton Fadiman

How To Do It: At least once a month, accompany your student to the local library. Combine this visit with their daily homework time if it's convenient. Stay for at least one hour, and during that time be a good model for library behavior by searching for, finding, and checking out books yourself. Support your student's library skills by involving them in the search for books you are checking out.

Make sure they know how to use the library. Familiarize them with the various parts of the library and show them how to use the services of the librarian and their assistants. If you are a bit rusty on some of these topics, seek help. It wouldn't hurt to introduce yourselves to one of the librarians and start to build a relationship. Don't be embarrassed if you need assistance. Ask for help together, and you will be setting a good example of how to make the most of a library. Remember, you needn't know everything about libraries to be a good role model. You just need to let your kid see you profit from your visit and enjoy yourself.

Enroll your youngster in after-school, summer, and holiday activities at your local library. Most libraries have readings, speakers, workshops, and book signings that are fertile ground for capturing a kid's imagination. Get on the mailing list, and make sure you are aware of upcoming events that might intrigue you or your student. Then make sure you attend.

Pitfalls: Library visits often suffer because it takes time to get both of you to the library and back. Avoid this trap by combining a quick bite at your favorite restaurant with the library visit. You can also save time by having your youngster do their homework at the library. As a matter of fact, this is a very good habit to develop. Libraries are wonderful places to do homework.

7

Take Charge
By Building An Educational Network With The Schools

Everyone has to deal with the schools and the people who run them. This can be done from a distance, or it can be done close up and personal. The relationships can be built on trust and friendship, or suspicion and anger. It's all up to you. Use this chapter to go beyond just dealing with the schools. Your commitment to your youngster requires more. Build a network of individuals who recognize your needs and are motivated to meet them.

Behave as a Most Valued Customer

Rationale: Many businesses today have transformed their sales and market-share by refocusing attention on the customer. They've found that the customer is the goose that lays the golden egg. A zealous effort to meet customer needs has produced unprecedented profits and benefits for everyone involved.

Likewise, enlightened schools recognize that they exist to meet your needs. You and your student are the primary focus for all their activities. You are their customers, and it's in everyone's interest for you to help them zealously meet your needs.

"The customer may not always be right, but they're always the customer."

Sales Proverb

Educators who treat you as a valued customer respect you. They see you as a precious resource. They recognize that schools are involved in a service industry and that everyone's success depends upon your satisfaction. Teachers and principals who don't treat you in this fashion set everyone up for failure.

As people who recognize their significance, the demeanor you and your young person adopt is pivotal. You can help educators treat you as the valued customer that your are, or you can be seen as a pain in the behind. Your approach will make all the difference in how educators see you. Assuming that you are a most prized customer and acting upon that belief makes it easy for educators to treat you in the way you deserve.

Behaving like a valued customer allows you to be very selfish. You needn't be concerned with what the school does for the kid down the block who needs special remedial attention, or even the kid next door who gets all A's and requires a challenge. Being a customer frees you from all considerations but those that impact you. It's the school's job to juggle the conflicting demands of its varied customers. It's your job to make sure they meet your kid's needs!

This doesn't mean you don't care about the others—you do. You fully expect that the schools will meet their special and individual needs as well. But when you're interacting with the schools as a customer, there's only one kid—*yours!*

This kind of attitude is not presumptuous. It's not expecting too much, nor is it some kind of "holier than thou" game. It's simply a matter of building a productive relationship between you and the schools. It's an effort to help the whole educational process get better, and it's the only attitude and approach that's appropriate for a Learning Ally.

A school that recognizes you as the **customer** will listen to you, will act upon your desires, and probe you for more information. They know your satisfaction is paramount to their success. They treat the contacts you make as opportunities, not interruptions. They make you feel like a team member, not an outsider. They give you what is rightfully yours.

Parents and students have the right:

▲ To be treated as a valued customer.
▲ To have their needs met 100% of the time.
▲ To have their inquiries dealt with as opportunities, not interruptions.
▲ To be informed in a timely and consistent manner.
▲ To operate in an environment of mutual respect.
▲ To be members of the team, not outsiders.

How To Do It: Behaving as a valued customer requires you to communicate three things to educators:

▲ Tell them you are the customer.

▲ Tell them how you want to be treated.

▲ Tell them about your educational goals.

You needn't be an expert in assertiveness to help educators develop this relationship. You just need to take the words I give you and personalize them.

For instance, to tell teachers and principals that you are the customer, use words like these:

"You know, Mr. Hobbs, I'd really like you to consider me the best customer of your educational services. I'm committed to letting you know what I need, and anything I can do to support you—let me know."

"Mr. Hobbs, I'm really pleased that you'll be providing our educational services. I know our tax dollars are being well spent in your class."

"Mr. Hobbs, I'm convinced the best relationship for you and me is as customer and supplier. You're the supplier of high quality educational services and Todd and I are your customers. What do you think?"

The best way to communicate how you want to be treated is to be direct and simple. Tell educators you and your student want to be treated in a fashion that meets three criteria: you want to be informed, empowered, and respected.

You might say something like this:

"Mr. Hobbs, as your customer, I feel I have the right to expect regular, timely information about Todd's performance. I'd like to have a significant role in helping him learn and I want this to happen in an atmosphere of mutual respect between us all. What do you think?"

"Here's my idea, Mr. Hobbs—see what you think about it. The way I see it, you, Todd, and I will work as a team. We're all obligated to keep the others posted as to any and all important events, and we'll treat each other with the respect and consideration due a teammate."

"Mr. Hobbs, I see Todd and me as your primary customers. I think that earns us the right to be informed, empowered, and respected. What do words like that mean to you?"

Finally, you must help educators see what you want as their customer. Tell them, straight out, what your goals are.

"Mr. Hobbs, Todd and I have set some goals for the year. We'd really be interested in your comments. First of all, he should turn in all assignments complete and on time. Secondly . . ."

"I'd really like your reaction to this, Mr. Hobbs. What would you say if I told you Todd and I had set a goal of having him reading at grade level performance by the end of the year?"

"Todd and I have agreed that goals are essential to high achievement, and consequently have developed three that we feel are particularly important. Would you look at these goals and comment on how you will be able to support them?"

Pitfalls: Many large bureaucratic organizations such as schools have gotten into some bad habits. They've forgotten who the customer is. They've gotten into the habit of telling the customer (students and parents) what they should want. Parents and students have played a part in this problem as well. They've let the schools and assorted educational experts lead them by the nose into the problems that often exist today—a system that works quite well for some students and fails miserably for others.

It's not your job to attack the system and make it pay for its failures and blunders. It's your job to help it become a better supplier of educational services to you, the **customer.** Do this by becoming a partner in the process, by making friends with the very people who've treated you as something less than a customer. You won't do it by becoming an adversary or an enemy.

Being the most important person in the education loop doesn't give you license to be abusive or heavy-handed. On the contrary, you need to be even more understanding and diplomatic. You must recognize that constantly focusing on your needs and goals is a formidable task. Holding educators responsible for satisfying your needs is what's expected. So is helping them to do it.

Recognize that "customer service" is a new concept for many educators. The private school systems have dealt with these pressures for years. It's now time to move the concept into the public arena. You may find you need to be firmly patient while your educators go through the transition. Change like this is often evolutionary, not revolutionary.

Conference with the Teacher Each Month

Rationale: When you meet with your child's teacher on a regular basis, you do two very important things. First, you collect timely, accurate data about the latest developments at school. Secondly, you build a constructive, friendly partnership that secures your kid a prominent place in the teacher's consciousness.

Too often we have these parent/teacher conferences after the fact. We hear about problem situations long after anything constructive can be done. Others have already interpreted the events, and the conference simply becomes your chance to get the bad news and try to do some damage control. There is no replace-

"The best argument is that which seems merely an explanation."

Dale Carnegie

ment for the raw data you get by meeting frequently with teachers. It's the only kind of information that will let you nip problems in the bud and make things happen, rather than simply respond.

Once you've established this constructive partnership, your kid is elevated on that teacher's list of priorities. Your youngster is no longer one of many students. She is now "special" and will get special attention because you've increased the stakes by building a partnership with the teacher. When that teacher looks at your kid they see more than just another student. They see you as well. Your presence makes it imperative that they succeed in teaching your student. This is so because success in meeting the needs of your kid is also success in achieving mutual goals the teacher has set with an adult who means something to them. They don't want to let you down, and they won't!

How To Do It: First of all, be prepared. Know what you want to discuss with your kid's teacher. In the absence of any real problems, ask two general questions about your kid's performance:

▲ What's working?

▲ What needs to be worked on?

You can always ask these questions because they give you the data that can most directly be put to use by you and your kid in your own efforts at home. Everyone is doing something right. What is it, and how can we make sure it continues? Conversely, what's not going so well, and what alternatives can we come up with that'll work better?

Other key questions are:

▲ What is my kid doing well in right now?
▲ What are you doing to challenge him?
▲ What is she doing that needs improvement?
▲ What are you doing to remedy the situation?

▲ What resources are there for help?
▲ What are your goals for my student?
▲ How are you going about achieving them?
▲ Are there any learning problems you are aware of?
▲ Is he getting along socially?
▲ How can I help?

Once you know what questions you're going to ask, make an appointment for a conference. Do this by contacting the teacher personally or phone the school secretary. Any school worth its salt will be more than willing to accommodate your wishes. If not, see the section in this chapter on making trouble, because failure to meet your needs in this area is a serious breach of the school's commitment to you and your student.

Your first conference should take place sometime during the first three weeks of school. At this meeting inform the teacher that you intend on meeting once a month for the whole year. Tell them you want to build a friendly partnership that will support your child's best work. Use words like these:

"Thanks for seeing me so promptly, Ms. Dade, I really appreciate it. My goal is to have a meeting like this on a monthly basis throughout the year. That way I can stay informed on Scott's progress and I can support you in any way you might need. How does that sound to you?"

Ms. Dade should agree wholeheartedly, and be more than willing to meet you on this frequent basis. She may suggest that all the conferences need not involve her, and that's perfectly OK. Your student most likely has several teachers. In the absence of problems you need only meet with one per month, but the majority of your meetings should be with your child's primary teacher or the teacher in whose class they are most challenged.

Take an active part in these meetings. Be prepared to talk about 50% of the time, but be willing to listen 75% of the time. The data you gather will generally be more useful to you than the data you give out. Recognize that teachers, principals, and specialists are educational experts. They deserve to be listened to and their advice, in most cases, should be taken. On the other hand, never forget that you are the *customer!* You have the right to be satisfied with any and all decisions.

Remember, this conference is a fifty-fifty deal. Be prepared to answer some questions about your student's life outside of school. Be prepared to give the teacher answers to questions like these:

▲ How much time does your kid spend in front of the TV?

▲ Are there any current health problems that could affect their learning?

▲ Is there anything going on in the family that might affect their learning?

▲ Is there anything going on in their relations with friends and peers that might affect their learning?

▲ Do they like school? How do they talk about school or specific teachers?

▲ How do you support their learning at home?

▲ Do they have responsibilities, a job, or family duties? If so, how are they performing?

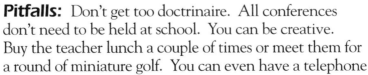

Pitfalls: Don't get too doctrinaire. All conferences don't need to be held at school. You can be creative. Buy the teacher lunch a couple of times or meet them for a round of miniature golf. You can even have a telephone conference in emergencies, as long as the majority of your conferences are face to face. Remember, your goal is to gather data that allows you to nip problems in the bud. You are also building a partnership that elevates your kid to a priority concern for their teacher.

Make Friends with Your Kid's Teacher

Rationale: Teachers who are friends with you as well as your kid will be more committed and do a better job. There's simply more in it for them to succeed. Not only do they help a child, they fulfill the expectations of a good friend and fellow adult.

Very little has ever been accomplished by attacking or bullying a teacher. This only breeds defensiveness on the part of a good person who is already under siege. Give your teachers a break. Be their friend and ally. Work at it even if you don't think they deserve it, because you're being friendly as much for yourself and your child as you are for them. If you're successful, everyone wins!

"The only way to have a friend is to be one."

Ralph Waldo Emerson

Make the teacher's payoff a new positive friendship with an adult who respects what they do and supports them in the process. More than anything, teachers are looking for recognition of the fine work they do. Give it to them in a friendly way.

How To Do It: Use the "show and tell" method when you set out to build a friendship with your kid's teacher.

1. <u>*Show*</u> **them you want to be their friend by doing these things:**

   ▲ *Have the teacher over to your home for dinner two times during the school year.* Do this once in early fall and once in early spring. Don't talk about school very much. Make it a social event. Inviting them to a party doesn't count. You have to sit down and share a meal. This is a rare opportunity for the teacher to really observe and understand your child in their own environment.

   ▲ *Send them at least four thank-you notes during the year.* Thank them for taking time with your kid or compliment them on some aspect of their program. Be positive and sincere.

   ▲ *Give your teacher a gift at Christmastime and at the end of the school year.* These don't have to be extravagant presents. Maybe something they could share with the rest of the students would be appropriate—a room decoration or food.

   ▲ *Volunteer your time to help out in the classroom.* Do this even if you have very little time to spare. Find some time to give, because it's a powerful message of goodwill on your part.

2. <u>*Tell*</u> them you want to be friends by saying these things:

▲ *Tell them you would really like it if you two could be friends.*

▲ *On a regular basis, tell them how much you appreciate their efforts.* Be specific about what you like, for example, taking the time to be certain Brenda has her homework assignment before she leaves each day.

▲ *Tell them about yourself.* Share your experience and values with them.

▲ *Tell them about your kid.* Tell them about your goals, your concerns, your dreams.

▲ *Tell them how much you value their friendship and what a positive effect it has had on you and your youngster.*

Pitfalls: Don't worry about being insincere or a phoney just because you choose to make friends with someone who can benefit your kid. You needn't make more of this relationship than is merited. Think of it as a business or work friendship. There are many relationships of this kind that serve as much a business purpose as they do a social one. As long as you are honest and sincere in your actions, you can be confident that you aren't trying to manipulate anyone. After all, we can all use more friends. Why not have that friend be your child's teacher?

If your kid has multiple teachers, it may be difficult to do all the things I suggest with each one. Choose the teacher or teachers who are most important to your child's success and concentrate your attention on them. There's nothing that says you can't have several teachers over for dinner at one time, or that you can't sit down and write a handful of notes at once. It's a greater challenge, but none the less imperative to be friends with all these people.

Suspend Your Belief in "Bad Teachers"

Rationale: Anytime you believe your kid has a "bad teacher" you are handicapping yourself. You reduce your options to a very short list when bad-teacher becomes the answer to all these questions: Why is my kid bored? Why won't she do her homework? Why are there notes coming home about disruptive behavior? Why does she fail?

The bad-teacher conclusion is so enticing that it often rules out any other possibilities. It simplifies things so well that it becomes addictive. You get hooked on an irrational vision of problems as people, rather than a more realistic perception of problems as people's *behavior.*

Most of us are pretty well stuck with who we are. When others judge us or demand that we become someone else, we react defensively and with anger. We resent being the "problem," and will spend all our energy trying to convince people the problem lies somewhere else. This is exactly what so-called

"As for an authentic villain, the real thing, the absolute, the artist, one rarely meets him once in a lifetime. The ordinary bad hat is always in part a decent fellow."

Collette

"bad teachers" do. They spend far more time trying to convince people they aren't bad than they do improving the situation.

Suspending belief in the bad-teacher means you've decided that your kid's education is more important than making someone admit that they are incompetent. Truly bad teachers will never admit it anyway, so don't even try—it's wasted effort. Use your energy to change something you have a little influence over—***their behavior!***

When most of us talk of a bad-teacher, we are saying that we don't feel they do their job very well. They appear not to have the proper skills or they refuse to use them. These teachers don't get the kind of results that we commonly expect from someone in their position. Certainly they aren't getting the results our teachers got from us! We draw this conclusion because our kids are

turned off about learning. They don't come home praising the virtues of their teachers; in fact, there is a lot of whining, complaining, and sarcasm. Most young people know when they are being shortchanged. They know which teachers are confident and competent, and they know who is just getting by or being forced to fill in a position required by the curriculum.

Kids who have good teachers like and respect them. They come home telling stories of the classroom. They rant and rave about how hard one is and how weird the other is. They aren't always positive or complimentary, but there is a clear level of respect present. If pushed, they'll admit that the good (but hard, or weird, or strict) teacher probably has their best interest in mind and does a pretty good job.

On the other hand, the badmouthing that accompanies poor teaching is much more pointed. It's direct and it's accompanied with terms of derision and sarcasm that are supported by examples and stories. Sometimes it lacks focus, but rarely does it lack negative emotion and a strong sense of betrayal. This kind of talk makes it very easy to believe your kid has a bad teacher. ***Suspend that thought.***

How To Do It: When you're pretty sure this is the case with your kid and their teacher, resist the bad-teacher trap. Choose to do something that helps the instructor meet your kid's needs. Remember that personal attacks and behind-the-scenes slander only increase the chances of your kid losing out. Your kid's attitudes and reactions will mirror your own, so take the position that there are no bad teachers. Act on the belief that there are only teachers who presently aren't meeting your expectations.

The vast majority of teachers are fully capable of educating your kid. They've all spent years in school developing their expertise and being certified. Recognize that it's more likely that something is happening that is keeping them from using that skill with your kid. Suspending the belief in their incompetence lets you search for the catalyst that will allow them to meet your kid's educational needs.

Start by listening to your kid's stories and believing what she says. Ask her to tell you about school. Don't assume that all kids hate it. Good teaching makes that very difficult. Expect that your kids will enjoy school and that they'll bring you tales of challenge, wonder and excitement. When they don't, resist the knee-jerk response of attacking the teacher. Find out what is going on before you jump to any conclusions.

Avoid the bad-teacher trap by collecting data of your own. Usually your concerns revolve around two complaints:

▲ My kid is being forced to do things that aren't effective.

▲ My kid is being prevented from doing things that are.

Take the time to be clear just what it is that you want added or removed from you youngster's learning environment. Then take those impressions to the teacher. Don't be afraid to tell educators about your concerns. You'd be surprised at how often even the best schools have to respond to inquiries such as this, and you'd also be surprised at how eager they are to meet your needs when you come with specific concerns rather than complaints about a bad teacher. Use words like these:

"Hi, Mr. Integer. Thanks for getting back to me so quickly. I called because I'm concerned about Gene's performance in math. His scores have declined rapidly this past session and he doesn't feel that he's been able to get as much help as he has in the past. I'd really like to sit down and talk about his performance with you and also get an opportunity to observe the whole math operation on a typical day. Is there a time in the next week that we could get together?"

Pitfalls: Yes, it's helpful to stop believing in bad teachers. But not entirely! In a very small percentage of situations the person teaching your kid may actually **be** a bad teacher. That is, they are a person who has no business being in contact with your kid, or any other kid, for that matter. In my years of teaching, I have to say I've seen a few.

The people I'm talking about fundamentally diminish the children they come in contact with. They are people who consciously or unconsciously betray the trust of children in a variety of ways. They hurt and abuse students as a by-product of their own personal problems. The damage they inflict runs from subtle neglect and sarcasm to verbal abuse and full-blown acts of criminal predation. We've all heard the stories and seen the reports on TV. This kind of outrage really exists and we risk our children's future by ignoring evidence that it's going on.

Only open, direct confrontation in this kind of situation will get to the truth. Don't hesitate if you think there is more going on than just a conflict of personalities or learning/teaching styles. Listen well and trust your child's and your own instincts. If you think your kid is suffering unduly at the hands of a teacher, start asking some questions and making some noise, immediately!

Don't worry about hurting anyone's feelings. If you truly have concerns about your young person's welfare, no good teacher would ever hold it against you for intervening on their behalf. Express your concerns and fears, then demand prompt, direct action.

Visit Your School for One Full Day, at Least Once a Year

Rationale: One strategy that's being used to improve our educational system is the business/school partnership. Local businesspeople and teachers in a large American city were paired in hopes that they could jointly come up with creative solutions to the problems that plagued the schools. Initially there was considerable fear on the part of the teachers that the business folks would just barge in and take over.

"A guest sees more in an hour than the host in a year."

Polish Proverb

146

The educators were worried that the business people would take a simpleminded approach that assumed everything could be easily fixed if the schools just implemented some hard-nosed management principles. The business contingent, for their part, were prepared to resist what they felt would be a patronizing attitude on the part of teachers. They weren't about to submit to a bunch of learning theory and academic jargon. What both groups found out surprised them.

To a person the teachers and the business people were surprised by how impressed they were with each other. The more time they spent together, the more they respected and admired each other. The businesspeople were shocked at how well the teachers managed a myriad of demands and variables at one time, while the teachers and administrators were impressed with the ability of the business contingent to see through the haze of data and identify root problems.

Walls of misconception are broken down in meetings like these. Fallacies are destroyed and the foundation for a real partnership between educators and the people they serve is built. The opportunity to see your teacher(s) and school in operation for a whole day allows you to collect data that's unavailable from any other source. Seeing the general flow of the day and how students and faculty interact sets you up to make the best decisions about your kid's education. You're no longer peeking through the window of parent conferences or report cards. You now are basing impressions on firsthand experience.

How To Do It: Call your youngster's teacher or the school principal and simply tell them you'd like to spend the whole day observing. Make sure you let them know what you want to gain from this visit. Reassure them that you aren't looking for dirt, you just think that this is the best way for you to understand the learning environment and how your student operates within it. Let them know your ultimate goal is to use the knowledge you gain to support your child's education at home.

Insist upon spending the whole day, start to finish. Don't let anyone talk you into less time. Be firm! Understand that visits of this kind can be stressful for everyone involved, and that there is a natural tendency to want to get it over with as soon as possible. But don't let the visit get abbreviated. ***Visit for the whole day!***

You might send a note that reads something like this:

"As you know, I've made a considerable commitment to helping Joel with his schoolwork this year. I feel I could be of much greater help if I knew in detail what his life is like at school. Consequently I'd like to visit for one full day to get a thorough sense of the content and flow of a typical day at school.

"Would you please check your schedule and propose a couple of days in the next few weeks that I might observe? I would like them to be typical days rather than special (field-trip, concert, assembly) days so that my impressions are realistic."

Once you've set up a day, prepare for it by making some notes of things you especially want to see and people you'd like to meet. You needn't spend the entire day in the presence of your student. You can wander around and look at the facility. You can meet people like the librarian or the counselor on an informal basis while they are actually doing their job. Don't, however, expect them to have an impromptu conference with you. Your job is to observe everything. Talk to the janitors and the cooking staff. Pay your respects to the principal, and be sure to make friends with the school secretary!

Don't be surprised if they put you to work. Having a body in the back of the room staring and making notes will cause anyone some stress. Most teachers rectify this by asking the visitor if they want to get involved. You may be enlisted to help a group work on an activity or be asked to read with a student. Regardless of how you help, getting involved is much more instructive and a lot less boring than sitting in the back taking notes. So jump on the opportunity if offered or volunteer if your help isn't requested.

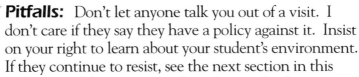

Pitfalls: Don't let anyone talk you out of a visit. I don't care if they say they have a policy against it. Insist on your right to learn about your student's environment. If they continue to resist, see the next section in this chapter on making trouble. It's your right to be involved in your kid's education.

Then again, don't forget to allay their fears. You are at school looking for things that will help **you** help your kid. Let the people at the school know that you are supportive and positive about what you want to achieve.

Be especially tuned in to your young person's reaction. At times, kids can be very embarrassed by the adults in their life. It's not fair and it's certainly not warranted, but it's a fact just the same. Don't let this stop you! Outline your plans with your young person first. Explain to them your motives and goals, and then listen to their reactions. Don't panic if they're not initially punchy with delight over the prospects. Calmly respond to their concerns and stick by your guns. Assure them you won't destroy their social standing for all time. Describe in detail just what you plan to do and what it'll look like. Assure them that you're only talking about a brief period of time. In most cases this will do the trick. Most students, after an initial period of weirdness, really enjoy having their folks in class. They end up being quite proud of them and enjoy the attention.

If your kid really goes off the deep end, you might reconsider the length of the visit, but not the visit itself. It may be necessary to structure a low-profile observation that doesn't draw too much attention to your kid. Some creative options might be observing classes your child isn't in for part of the time. Maybe you could schedule a few conferences during the day or leave for part of the time. Try to be firm, positive, and confident, while at the same time keeping a realistic eye on the level of your child's resistance.

In the end, your relationship as an ally in your child's learning is more important than any data you can collect in a school visit. If your plan to visit threatens that relationship, dump the plan and start working on building enough trust so that a visit will be possible in the future.

Make Trouble Without Being a Troublemaker

Rationale: As important as it is to have a good relationship with your child's teacher, occasionally you will need to cause problems, to be a major thorn in that same teacher's side. You'll do this because you refuse to put your concern for the teacher ahead of your child's learning.

When this happens—and it's guaranteed to happen if you're operating as a Learning Ally—you must be prepared to hold your teacher/friend's feet to the fire and make them produce for your child. It will be necessary for you to demand things that make life very hard for your child's teacher.

You will require this teacher to give the kind of support and instruction that is logistically beyond their ability (at least in terms of the way schools are run now). In fact, there will be times when you will require things that are patently impossible, and yet you'll go right ahead and make these demands because the comfort and sanity of the teacher is not your primary concern. Your child's education is!

You will ask the teacher to do things for your student that probably rob other kids of their instruction time. You're going to put this teacher, this friend of yours, in a very tight spot. The demands you make on them, as an ally of your child's learning, will literally back them into a corner. You will feel badly about doing this, but you'll go ahead and do it.

It's undeniable that the system we have for educating our kids is in need of repair. In many places it's on the verge of collapse. The reason it doesn't collapse is because it's being propped up by committed, talented, and well-intentioned educators. Your child's teacher is probably putting in extra time right now to "bandage" that wounded system. Yet the heroics of teachers can't correct the problems of most school systems. Teachers don't have the power.

Unfortunately they are directly in the line of fire of unhappy parents, the business community, and politicians. Teachers feel the pain generated by this breakdown. They feel it more frequently and intensely than almost anyone else. Anyone else, that is, except those kids who are falling through the cracks of a failing system. These children's loss is simply more important and less tolerable, and that's why you must make trouble on occasion.

Your responsibility as a Learning Ally is to your youngster. The pressure you put on members of the present system is not a primary concern. Your goal is to get your kid's needs met 100% of the time—nothing less. Have faith that the pain you cause your teacher today will ultimately support initiatives to improve the way kids are educated in the future.

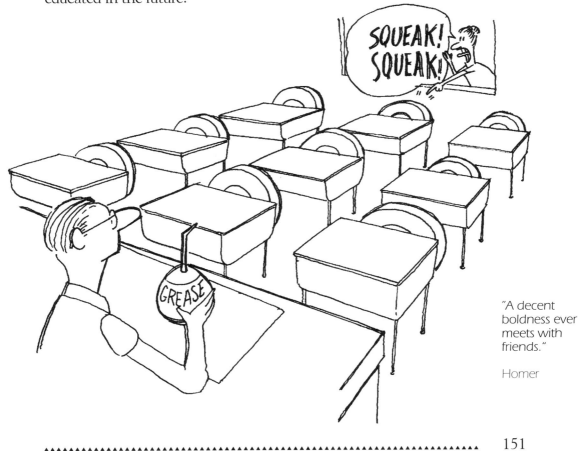

"A decent boldness ever meets with friends."

Homer

151

As a teacher I find this is difficult advice to give. Classroom teachers don't need any more pressure, regardless of how well-intentioned it is. They haven't enough time now to create all the miracles expected of them. I wonder how they could survive if everyone started pushing the system in this fashion. The answer is, they couldn't. They and the rest of the educational system would have to come up with a better way, a way that doesn't require such unfair sacrifices of its teachers. That's my hope.

How To Do It: Few of us would characterize ourselves as troublemakers, but that's often the feeling we get when we push the system to produce for our kids. We are frustrated and angry because our normal avenues of communication have failed and it seems like valuable time is passing and nothing is being done. Don't be afraid to push the system. Your judgment is probably right.

Generally there are two levels of troublemaking, gentle prods or *requests,* and forceful *demands.*

1. Request a meeting and follow through.

If you have done your best to make your needs known through the normal avenues of good communication that you've established with the schools, but haven't received satisfaction, it's necessary to make a more formal request. State this request in the form of a plea for assistance, an "I need your help" statement. Do it first in a note or letter that outlines your needs. Follow up with a face-to-face meeting to reinforce your seriousness.

Writing a note is key to making requests work. It gives the schools warning of your frustration and it allows them to prepare to meet your needs. The vast majority of your problems are a result of the teacher being unaware of the situation or unprepared to help you. The note will greatly improve your chances of satisfaction.

Always follow up with a personal meeting so you can verbally restate your "I need your help" statement. Follow through with the meeting even if you think the problem is being solved. It's a great opportunity to give the schools some positive feedback and thanks.

Here's an example:

"I really need your help in dealing with a problem Trent is having in geography. It seems he is frustrated with the kind of tests the class is given. Even though he studies and feels he knows the material, his grade is often a C or at times lower. He tells me there are "trick questions" that make it hard to do well. I don't know if this is true or not, but when I've helped him study he seems to know all the facts on your prep-sheet.

"As you might remember, I mentioned this concern in our last meeting and you said you'd look into it. Since there hasn't been any real change, I'd like to set up a time when we could meet to figure out what to do. I'm really worried about Trent's motivation in geography. Please give me a call at your earliest convenience."

The meeting you request is merely an opportunity to send the clear message that you are serious about your concern, and to eliminate any misconceptions. Be friendly and focus your attention on the situation. Remember, you are trying to fix the problem, not the blame!

2. Demand a meeting and follow through.

Probably 90% or more of problems can be dealt with through requests. When they fail, it's time to get much stronger in your approach. You must demand what is rightfully yours, and do it in a fashion that is constructive. Do this by describing what is now unacceptable and what satisfactory alternative you want it replaced with. Again, make your point first in writing and follow up with a meeting. You may also move up the chain of command at this point by sending copies to the principal or the board.

Here's an example:

"This letter is to inform you of a situation that is unacceptable to me. My son, Trent, is presently earning a D+ in your geography class. He is getting this grade in spite of the hours of study I have observed and the help I've personally given him in preparing for tests.

"You and I have discussed this situation on a number of occasions (Oct. 3, Nov. 28, Dec. 12) and I was expecting the improvement Trent is capable of by now. The fact is, though, there has been no improvement.

"Please call me to set up a time for a meeting. I would like this meeting to include you and me, as well as the principal and Trent. I fully expect that we will leave this meeting with a plan to improve my son's performance."

3. Be polite.

Just because you are making demands does not mean you must take an adversarial position. On the contrary, the only way you'll get a lasting solution is to get the educators on your side. Don't alienate them by being a jerk. Be firm, polite, and friendly. Demonstrate your commitment by reading your original letter or restating the contents. Be an active member of this conference and help your youngster give his or her side of the story without feeling overwhelmed by the adults in the room. Make it clear you intend to leave with solutions that are constructive alternatives to the present unacceptable situation.

 Pitfalls: Don't lose heart. Confrontation is never easy, especially when you are in a conflict with a person you admire and trust. Remember that situations like these are inevitable and are most often due to poor communication or information, not evil people. As a Learning Ally you are obligated to deal with them when the time comes.

Don't enter this arena unprepared. Make sure you have the data that supports your contentions and make sure you are ready to present it. You may need to practice a few of your lines with a friend or in front of a mirror. Do whatever is necessary to feel comfortable in making your points. You don't have to be smooth, but you do need to be prepared.

8

Take Charge
Of Technology

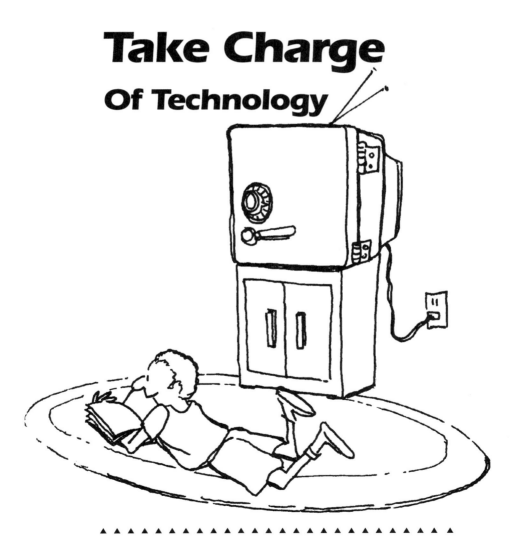

▲▲▲▲▲▲▲▲▲▲▲▲▲▲▲▲▲▲▲▲▲▲▲▲▲▲▲▲▲▲▲▲

The question isn't whether everything coming out of the television is wholesome for young minds. The question is whether television offers anything worthwhile at all! Is the passive nature of this kind of medium just too debilitating, or does it all depend on the kid? Use this chapter to determine what kind of support you'll give to the viewing of television.

Computers are a different story. Where most people are automatically skeptical and negative about television, they are overly accepting and positive about computers. This chapter will help you sift through some of the hype about computers so you can decide if one makes sense for your young person.

Get Rid of Your Television Set

Rationale: All television programming is bad for your kid. Even the best educational material requires your youngster to passively sit and watch. Television teaches kids that "watching" is more fun, interesting, and easy than "doing." It erodes many kids' self-confidence by portraying beautiful, glamorous people living unrealistic life-styles that can never be approximated in real life. Because they are convinced they can never achieve the performance of their idols, a lot of kids opt to sit and watch the tube rather than go out and tackle life themselves.

The people who produce most television programming don't care if your kid succeeds in school. They only care about what products he or she buys. They will do anything to promote their products, including undermining your youngster's education. As long as your kid sits in front of the tube, there is little you can do to diminish this negative influence. Media people are much more sophisticated and adept at human manipulation than you are. You

"It is television's primary damage that it provides ten million children with the same fantasy, ready-made and on a platter."

Marya Mannes

can't go head-to-head with them and win. They can garner all manner of data to prove that the shows running their commercials are good for your kid. In reality the only thing those programs are good at is molding your young people into consumers—uninformed and unquestioning ones at that!

As a Learning Ally, your goal is to support the development of a confident, educated young person. Television threatens that development. Its goals are exactly the opposite. Thus you must do everything possible to remove its influence from your kid's environment and fill the void with wholesome, challenging, real-life activities.

 **How To Do It:** The most direct way to accomplish this task is to remove all television sets from your home. Give them away, donate them to charity (although not to the schools), or just dump them. It's not important how you do it; just get all the TV sets out of your youngster's environment.

Removing the television set is not the hard part of this advice. It's filling that new free time formerly spent zombielike in front of the tube. Now you must come up with activities that are entertaining and support your kid's development. Can it be done? Yes. You aren't creating as much dead-time as you think. The television stole much more time than you might have thought from the necessary activities your kid was already involved in. Thus a good chunk of the newly created dead-time will be eaten up by normal at-home activities, like chores and homework. The rest of this newly created time will be filled with revolutionary activities like:

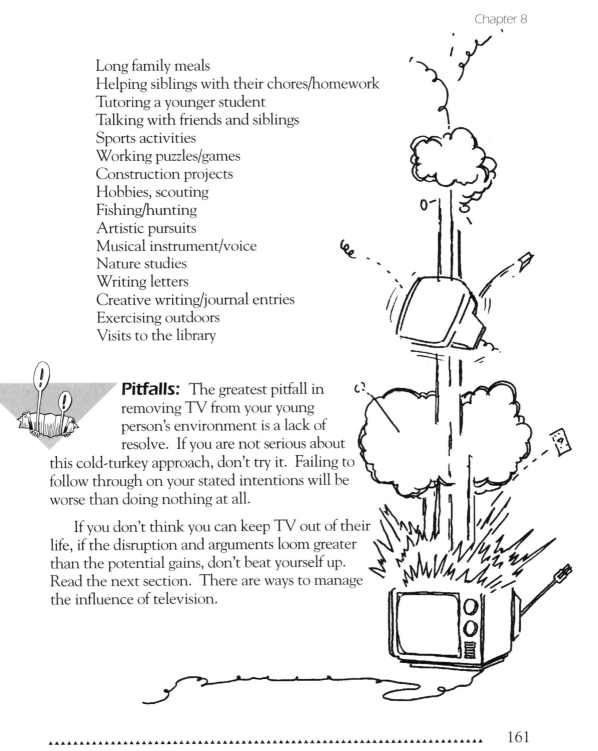

Long family meals
Helping siblings with their chores/homework
Tutoring a younger student
Talking with friends and siblings
Sports activities
Working puzzles/games
Construction projects
Hobbies, scouting
Fishing/hunting
Artistic pursuits
Musical instrument/voice
Nature studies
Writing letters
Creative writing/journal entries
Exercising outdoors
Visits to the library

Pitfalls: The greatest pitfall in removing TV from your young person's environment is a lack of resolve. If you are not serious about this cold-turkey approach, don't try it. Failing to follow through on your stated intentions will be worse than doing nothing at all.

If you don't think you can keep TV out of their life, if the disruption and arguments loom greater than the potential gains, don't beat yourself up. Read the next section. There are ways to manage the influence of television.

Use Your Television Wisely

Rationale: OK, so it's not possible to throw all your televisions away. What can you do, recognizing that you still have this electronic monster in your home and it's literally sucking the academic life from your kids? A lot, really, and most of the solutions are common-sense. Television is bad for your kid not because it's inherently evil. It's bad because kids watch too much television and they watch the wrong programs. All you need to do is get them involved in curtailing the amount of time they spend in front of the tube and then help them make better programming decisions.

AQUARIUM

BOOKSHELF

PUPPET THEATRE

COOL MASK

Changing your youngster's television habits is not as difficult as it may initially seem. They may look enthralled by that inane sit-com, but it really does no more for them than it does for you. Be assured that they would find much greater satisfaction doing something themselves than being an observer of someone else's activities. They simply don't have the experience or confidence to give it a try, and that's where you, the Learning Ally, can help.

How To Do It:

1. Jointly set a number of viewing hours that you and your young person can agree is an acceptable level. This will inevitably be a compromise, yet you can make up with quality viewing what you give up in quantity. Lobby for at least a 30% reduction in viewing to begin with. Also shoot for an agreement that they can choose $^2/_3$ of their programs and you will pick $^1/_3$.

2. Once you get agreement on the amount of viewing time, make your programming choices. Regardless of how horrible their selections are, resist criticism. You must show respect for their judgment if you want them to consider your preferences. Do some research and choose programs that promote activity, that teach some skill or ability. Short of "how-to" programming, opt for shows that take your young person out of their environment: out of doors, out of their town, out of their culture. Expose them to the widest array of people and things the world has to offer.

"Television is now so desperately hungry for material that they are scraping the top of the barrel."

Gore Vidal

3. Television viewing can be productive and enlightening if it's used to promote a dialog between you and your young person. Watch TV with them and afterward discuss the programs. Ask them questions about what they saw. Was it realistic? Were there certain values being presented? Do those values match yours? Was it a good or bad program? Why or why not? Often this kind of discussion between you and your kid can make the difference between an hour wasted and an hour well spent.

4. **Monitor and be selective about what you watch—at least the programs you watch in front of your youngster.** Remember, you are an influential role model. Watch the kind of programs you would like them to be viewing.

Pitfalls: Television can open doors like no other medium, but remember, it only opens doors. Eventually your young person has to start walking through some of those portals. They accomplish this by actively getting off the sofa and doing something. Make sure the passive activity of sitting and watching TV is the catalyst for your kid to do something energetic and wholesome.

Discourage the Viewing of Rock Videos

Rationale: Rock music videos are the equivalent of mental dioxin for young people. Sustained viewing will lobotomize them faster than you can say "Turn down that racket!" Most people who would be a Learning Ally have at one time or another enjoyed rock music. The problem arises when that rock music is combined with vivid, fast-paced, sexually supercharged images. The cocktail created by this mixture of sound and video is simply too potent. Instead of entertaining and enlightening kids, it overloads them with questionable values and premature sexuality. All of this is served up as art that is somehow representative of kids and how they feel. It isn't! It represents the financial interests of the people who make the rock videos. Not surprisingly, these interests are in conflict with your kid's development. The final destination they have in mind is pretty shortsighted.

That destination is most often a check-out stand where your kid will try to buy something that maintains the myth that they can become just like the people in the rock videos. The bottom line is that through continued watching of this poison, your youngster will become a pliant, eager, and worst of all, ignorant consumer. The unscrupulous marketers love it. They have a whole audience of kids who don't question the values and beliefs of their idols. They merely lust for products that are buoyed about on waves of sexuality and a strong rock beat.

Of course sexuality is natural and so is a strong rhythmic beat in music. Artistic expressions that incorporate these two things often touch us on a profound and primal basis. It appeals to that which is most fundamental in all of us. Yet when these same elements are used for a commercial motive rather than an artistic one, the outcome is far from wholesome.

"The trouble with us in America isn't that the poetry of life has turned to prose, but that it has turned to advertising copy."

Louis Kronenberger

Marketers know that kids aren't prepared to deal with this kind of input. The resulting confusion makes young folks easy prey. They aren't ready for the sexuality nor are they good at distinguishing fact from fantasy. Many kids really believe that these videos portray reality. Young girls especially get a wildly slanted view of their role in society, a role it's doubtful most parents would approve of or choose for their kids.

Rock music is fine—by itself. It can be a positive influence on kids. It can energize them and make them think. It can help them establish who they are and draw the lines between themselves and the adult world. Rock can do all of these things and more, if a young person just **listens** to it!

Video, TV, and movies are all fine. There is no comparable medium for portraying the dynamism and fluidity of life. We would all be poorer in some ways for their absence. Yet pairing these two immensely powerful media with sexually laced themes preys on our children. It exploits them because it uses its power to convince your kids that they are nothing if they don't adopt the same questionable values and buy the same superficial products used by the fantasy people it presents.

How To Do It:

1. Plan A: Don't let them watch rock videos!

No way! Rant and rave. Put your foot down. Simply forbid it. Throw an adult tantrum if you must, but convince them that you believe rock videos are not in their best interest; in fact you think they're poison. Let your youngster know that you believe anything short of this strong stance would be tantamount to reneging on your commitment as a Learning Ally.

2. Plan B: Recognize that maybe it's not entirely possible to cut off all access to rock videos, and maybe you don't want to be so heavy-handed anyway.

What can you do to send the message of concern to your kid? What can you do to help them understand the sinister goals behind this enticing form of sales (don't call it entertainment!)?

Sit down and watch a full hour of rock videos with your young person. Do it at a time when they would normally be watching, not when it's convenient for you. That way you'll be watching the material that your kid is really exposed to. Do this several times, maybe once after school and a couple of times in the evening or the morning.

Don't judge. Don't fume, rave, gag or pontificate on the material you're watching. Just sit down and watch an hour of rock videos with your young person. What you'll be doing during this time is collecting data, and some current data at that. Your young person will be there, too, so it'll be easier to agree upon what was seen. You don't want to get into a battle over what was in a particular video.

After you've jointly collected your data, discuss it together. Be up front about your concerns. Tell what you think. If you think rock videos are the equivalent of a do-it-yourself lobotomy, tell them. Be willing to listen to their opinions as well. Remember, it's also OK if they disagree with you. Be firm and calmly assured about your position. They will be duly impressed with your sense of confidence, and maybe even listen to what you have to say. Confidence is impressive to kids. They feel comfortable and safe around people who exude strong convictions. This is not to be confused with arrogance, which they hate and can spot a mile away.

Having viewed the tapes together, ask them some questions about what they've seen and heard. Some examples of good questions that will start them thinking about the value of these videos are:

▲ What do you think the message of Video X is?

▲ Can you remember any lyrics in particular? Do any words or phrases stand out?

▲ How were the women/men portrayed? What seemed to be the function or role of each sex?

▲ How were minorities represented?

▲ Is the video realistic? Does it portray real life?

▲ Did the video seem to support any position, political or cultural? What was it?

▲ Did the video attack any political or cultural positions or group of people you know of?

▲ What do you think they were trying to sell, if anything?

▲ What had more impact—the images, the music, or the lyrics?

▲ What could I, an adult, learn from this video?

▲ What do you think I'd object to in this video?

▲ What do you think I liked about it?

▲ What did you like or object to in the video?

▲ Do you think the lives of the people in the videos are really like they are portrayed? What must they be like?

The object of discussing the videos is to dissect and question them. With your help, kids can become better consumers of art as well as of marketing. They naturally question your authority. Help them challenge the authority that's disguised as counterculture.

Encourage your young person to "listen" to the music they like without someone else's readymade images. Challenge them to create images in their own mind that come from the music. True, active listening is a creative process. Your kid's mind needs to be engaged while listening and enjoying music, not passively hearing the music on TV and waiting to see the "correct" images.

This creative challenge appeals to kids. They're tired of being told what to think and see and experience. Many rebel against anything they feel is being rammed down their throat. Yet few question the dogma they're being fed by rock videos. Help them rebel against that, too! This could all end up being a great lesson in questioning authority. It's a skill all young people should develop because they are surrounded by so much authority, both legitimate and fraudulent. We've all done some of this questioning, sometimes to our profit and at times to our detriment. Help them get some practice in questioning an authority in their lives that really deserves the scrutiny.

Pitfalls: In your zeal to depict the evil of rock videos, don't set yourself up for failure by backing your young person into a corner. They can't understand or even listen to your point of view if they're forced to admit they're wrong first. Young people are not idiots for enjoying rock videos. However, they are being manipulated if they aren't questioning that electronic authority. Help them get that sharp-eyed skepticism by making opportunities for them to be right about the intentions and goals of rock videos.

Don't Panic if You Don't Own a Computer

Rationale: There's no reason to panic if you can't afford a computer. Access to a home computer isn't necessary to educational success. Computers aren't magic machines. They can't transform a poor achiever into a good student. They can't motivate an otherwise bored and lackadaisical student into a willing worker. The best and most powerful computer at your kid's disposal is the one sitting on top of their shoulders. Help them program that properly and they won't suffer from the lack of its electronic counterpart.

Many people purchase a computer with the belief that it's a do-everything machine—a magic pill that's going to transform their kid overnight. They're convinced that computers will succeed where everything else has failed. Of course they're wrong. Home computers are a risky bet if you're getting one in the hopes that your kid's performance will skyrocket.

Computers are powerful tools. They logically store, manipulate, and retrieve data at a phenomenal rate. They are very good at doing exactly what they are told to do. In fact, they do it to a maddening degree. Yet for all their power and speed, computers can't think for themselves or for your kid. They can't begin to make the decisions and judgments you make as you guide and support your youngster.

"Man is still the most extraordinary computer of all."

John F. Kennedy

Computers need to be directed by a user who is knowledgeable, who knows where she is going and how she is going to employ the computer to get there. In the absence of this direction, both computer and user are dead in the water. This is why it's a mistake to blindly dump a lot of money on computer gear for your kid without making sure they are able and willing to use it. You might as well buy them a heart-lung machine and hope it transforms them into a cardiologist.

Don't Panic if You Decide to Get a Computer

Rationale: It's been said that there will be two kinds of people in the next century, those who control computers and those who are controlled by computers. Kids who have hands-on access to computers are more likely to learn to command and utilize them than those kids who get only fleeting opportunities using the rare machine found in today's classroom.

Kids today seem to teach themselves about computers. They get a lot of knowledge by osmosis. Whether it's from the computer display at the department store or from playing games on their friend's, they already have an education of sorts in computers. The problem is that this education is rarely complete or accurate. Usually it's heavily weighted toward entertainment.

If your youngster has a computer of his own, he's much more likely to go beyond just the video game stage. He has the time and opportunity to call upon the computer to support him in academic pursuits. This will especially be true if you make sure the computer is a competent machine with a full range of educational software.

Computers are not a replacement for books or an excuse for not acquiring the educational fundamentals we all learned in the precomputing days. However, they do augment those skills. Computers can supercharge all of the good skills your student already has. They open up worlds of data to be manipulated. Using a computer supports good reading and math skills and then goes on to challenge kids in a fashion that uniquely meets their needs as young learners.

Computers challenge students in a totally nonjudgmental fashion. They don't register approval or disapproval. They don't get nervous or personally involved in the exercise. They are simply there presenting the problems or supplying the data. Your student can take risks with a computer that would be out of the question with a parent or peer. With computers it's easy for the youngster to go out on a limb, it's simple to make those wild creative guesses. And if they're wrong, the computer just waits for another try— no shame, no embarrassment. Computers help kids by making it OK to be wrong. When their fear of looking foolish diminishes, kids learn that the wrong answer is often a stepping stone to the right one.

"The real danger is not that computers will begin to think like men, but that men will begin to think like computers."

Sydney J. Harris

Computers can only help your kid if certain criteria are met. Before you invest in any system, make sure these conditions exist:

1. Your kid knows how to use the computer system you are getting them (or you know how and you can teach them).

2. Your student actually has work that the computer can help them do—word processing, math drill, geography drill, typing tutor, spelling games.

3. Your youngster wants to do their work with the aid of a computer—they are enthusiastic and excited about using the computer for more than just the games it can play.

If you can meet these three criteria, a computer is a good bet. It will support you in your efforts as a Learning Ally. But remember, it will never replace you!

How To Do It: Home computing has come within the financial range of most households. A system that will suffice for several or all of the school years is well within your means. You needn't buy a new computer and certainly not the most powerful one. You should, though, buy a relatively mainstream system that has an abundance of educational software available. This usually means an Apple or IBM-compatible machine, although there are several other computers that are lesser known yet still meet all the requirements. Check first with your student. What system do they use at school? It would be good, but not necessary, if your system matches what is used in the classroom.

Buying a computer can be a daunting experience. There are a myriad of decisions to be made. The best bet is to find a friend who is computer-literate (otherwise known as a computer nut) and ask them to aid you in your effort. Simplicity should be your guiding principle. You don't need a fancy system with all the bells and whistles. This may disappoint your computer-literate friend. Nevertheless, all you need is a computer, a monitor, and a printer, none of which needs to be cutting-edge technology.

Be sure to shop. If you don't you'll get stung. There can be major price differences from outlet to outlet, and savings of 50% and more from one to the other are commonplace. Here again your computer friend will help you distinguish between a deal and a come-on.

Once you've acquired the right computer system, your challenge begins: making sure it's used properly. Make sure the time your student spends on the computer is spent in these wholesome, scholastic pursuits:

Drill and practice programs
Word processing
Researching data bases
Writing programs
Educational/simulation games
Artistic/graphic programs

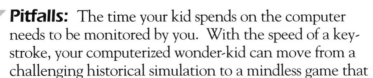

Pitfalls: The time your kid spends on the computer needs to be monitored by you. With the speed of a keystroke, your computerized wonder-kid can move from a challenging historical simulation to a mindless game that requires nothing more than hand-eye coordination. Check in frequently and keep a diligent eye on what they are doing on the computer. Try to catch them "doing right." Take every opportunity to reinforce appropriate use of this electronic tool.

9

Take Charge
By Leading The Team

MT. EDUCATION

Before schools, young people learned by working shoulder-to-shoulder with their elders. A young girl or boy might spend every waking hour in close proximity to their parent or other significant adult.

The kind of education this experience afforded was broader and more intimate than anything imaginable today. Kids learned their society's skills while constantly observing their mentor. Lessons were learned well because they were project-based. Whether the lesson was building a barn or taking part in the annual gathering of nuts and berries, theory was always combined with practice and application. Use this last chapter to give your young person the same advantage. Working shoulder-to-shoulder, they'll make you proud.

Hand-build Something Together

Rationale: At some point in every young person's life there comes the realization that people fall into two distinct categories: those who are controlled and molded by the forces of life, and those who mold and control those very same forces.

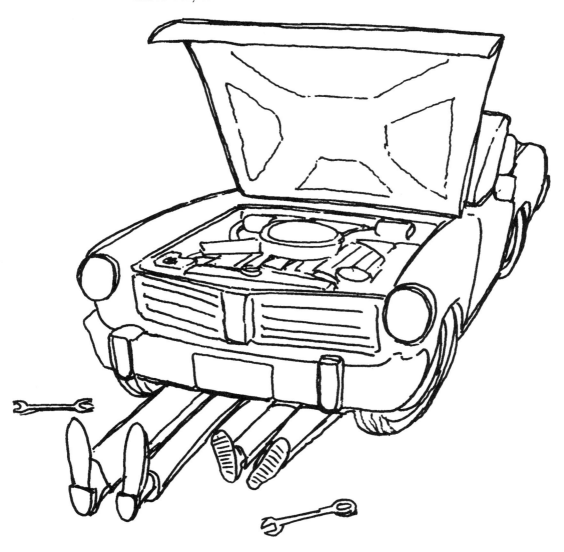

Kids categorize themselves based on their own very short history. Youngsters who've seen little challenge, who've been protected from life's trials and errors, often see themselves as helpless leaves blown about by the winds of chance. They see their role as one who must bravely line up and take whatever the world dishes out. Making the best of it, their common destiny is to wait. On the other hand, if that child's history is full of opportunities to bend, fold, and manipulate their surroundings, they will naturally treat the world in a similar fashion. Kid's with this confident sense of the world are doers. They decide to be the catalysts of life, rather than just one of the chemicals in its formula. Sure they get more bumps and bruises, but they also get a large share of life's rewards.

"We put our love where we have put our labor."

Ralph Waldo Emerson

Building things with their own hands gives kids the experience of being a catalyst. Hammering, weaving, gluing, carving, or sewing—all teach a kid that they are able to combine previously unrelated elements of this world and create something productive and useful. This kind of experience is an opportunity for a youngster to feel important and vital. Building things combines the practical experience and boosts in self-esteem that constitute an absolute elixir for academic success.

How To Do It: Choose a building project in which both you and your young person share an interest. It might be a hobby you'd like to share with your youngster. If so, remember that your role is to help your youngster build something themselves rather than to show them how an expert does it. You want them to see how a project progresses from the first stages of planning and material selection to assembly, troubleshooting, and finishing details. Throughout the process consider yourself their stagehand and mentor. The quality of the finished product is less important than the opportunity to build something with their hands, on their own.

The size of your project is not important. Kids can learn as much from crocheting a doily as they can from building a baseball diamond. What does matter is the logical sequence of events your kid needs to navigate in order to be successful. The experience of building something by hand will reinforce the principle that there are beginnings, middles, and ends to all efforts, and that disciplined effort is a key to achieving success.

Make the building project a challenge, even to the degree that your kid may not believe they can do it. Indeed, the best projects should be impossible without your help. Your role is to gently and unobtrusively help them in the construction until their skepticism turns into conviction. If you do your job right, you'll be rewarded with the words, "I didn't know I could do it! Thanks for the help, Mom."

Some suggested building projects are:

Model planes, cars, animals
Woodworking projects
Crocheting, needlepoint
Gardening
Puzzles
Home decorations, ornaments
Sewing/clothing design
Home construction/improvement
Model railroading
Woodcarving, whittling
Weaving/fabric design
Toll-painting/decoupage
Flower arranging

Boatbuilding
Auto repair
Drawing/painting
Electronics
Cooking
Fly-tying
Telescope-making
Jewelry-making
Lapidary
Paper-making
Origami
Kite-building
Bookbinding

Pitfalls: You may be saying, "But wait a minute. I'm not so hot with my hands and I've never really been into hobbies or home projects. How can I help my kid if I'm not an expert myself?" Don't panic, you don't have to be handy.

Being unhandy is actually an advantage. You're in a unique position to model the patient, step-by-step technique used by any neophyte in learning a new skill. Remember, kids are in this position all the time. Unlike adults, they haven't had the opportunity to carve out secure little niches where they feel proficient and comfortable. Let them see how brave you can be. Wade into those uncharted waters with your youngster in tow.

Get Your Student Involved in a Service Activity

Rationale: Kids who believe they are worthy, valuable people learn more and get better grades than kids who don't. This positive self-regard goes way beyond common conceit. It has nothing to do with being "cool" or popular. It has everything to do with your young person believing they make a difference and reaping the rich harvest of confidence and self-esteem that come from *being of service.*

"Nothing makes one feel so strong as a call for help."

George MacDonald

You can't teach a young person to have high self-esteem. You can't give it to them. All the compliments and hugs in the world can only lay the foundation. Your kids know you love them, and they know you'll say anything to try to help them. That's why it's hard for them to believe you when you tell them how great they are. They appreciate the sentiments but need some corroborating evidence of their value. Young people need to *earn* that high regard, and one of the best ways to earn it is to be of service to someone else who needs their help.

Young people have a consuming desire to grow up, to get on with life. They want direct experience of the world and they're willing to take the chances that experience requires. Their natural hunger for the realities of this world emboldens them. They want a taste of the adult world, and not just a safe, spoon-fed taste, but a pie-in-the-face mouthful. They need to test themselves and willingly accept the disturbing, frightening, and challenging aspects of whatever that exam requires.

The opportunity to be of service to other people is a powerful immersion in the world. It's never fake or trumped up. It capitalizes on a natural nobility in your child that compels them to help others, especially other kids. If you've watched children for any time at all, you know what great teachers they are. They give of themselves with simple ease, and manage to impart what they know without judgment or condescension. What's more, they do it all in a way that is gentle, fun, and effective.

Kids who have an opportunity to help others feel that they are a person of substance. They know they have something to offer, because they've done it. They've volunteered their services to the outside world and were taken up on the proposition. They helped someone in need, and in turn their own needs were met.

The opportunity to help others, who are often less fortunate in some way, teaches a profound lesson in life. Kids learn very quickly how much all people have in common. They overcome the natural fear of those who are different by getting close to them. The world of your youngster becomes a less threatening place, and they become more free to operate within it. Young people who are involved in service activities are increasingly convinced that they are people to be reckoned with. These kids believe in themselves and, in turn, take care of themselves. They make sure other people, like teachers and parents do, too! Youngsters who've been of service to others know they are worthy, and they do well in school because academic achievement is in line with the high regard they have for themselves.

How To Do It: Nurture that which is highest in your child by helping them help someone else. Find a way for your young person to get involved in a service organization. This can be in your community or neighborhood, or even in your own family. The activity of helping is more important than the environment.

Here are some situations that are especially powerful:

1. Service groups

Associating with other young people who are also involved in a service activity reinforces and validates the experience. Your kid makes important friendships with peers who have common values and goals. This reinforces their sense of belonging, which is of critical importance to young people.

2. Service through teaching

If your child can actually teach what they know to someone else, the experience will more readily support their achievement at school. Remember, no matter how poorly your kid does in school, he or she is a natural teacher, unconstrained by the hang-ups or training of adults. Kids are kinder and more open in their abilities to instruct. Give them a chance to teach what they know to a younger and less skilled person, and then watch both grow.

3. Partnerships

If you can work along with your young person in this activity, you'll be reinforcing your role as a Learning Ally. Sharing the responsibilities and effort sends the message that you believe what they are doing is meaningful. They interpret that message as "I am important and meaningful." When you reinforce what they do, it builds who they are.

Pitfalls: Don't let fear stop you! Don't let your own concerns and anxiety about serving others influence your child. Barge right ahead and don't worry about your suitability, commitment, or motivations. Your young person will follow your lead and will soon begin showing you the way.

On the other hand, there's nothing wrong with starting out conservatively. Visit the organizations or people you would like to be of service to. Ask questions, get training, do whatever it takes to help yourself take the plunge. When you're ready, grab your kid's hand and leap!

Give Your Youngster Daily Chores

Rationale: In today's world, kids suffer in a way that is entirely new. For the first time in history, young, vital people don't feel needed. They fail to see a productive role for themselves in the family or society. Unlike generations past, there's no farm that needs their unbounded energy and strength. There's no hunt that relies on their swiftness or keen eyesight. No event or person seems to depend on their performance, and kids are the poorer for it.

Efforts to protect and nurture young people go too far if they totally relieve kids of the chance to do meaningful daily work at home. With no genuine role for the youngster, the adult world says, "You aren't actually part of the real life going on around you. You are in a make-believe sort of world. A practice world. Try hard, anyway. Get a good education and have some fun along the way because, before you know it, the mundane pressures of adulthood will overtake you." With this kind of message, it's no wonder a lot of kids don't apply themselves. They see no goal, or if they do, it's so foggy and far off that there's little to get excited about.

Meaningful daily chores are the most direct way for your young person to develop self-esteem and a conviction that someone depends upon them. Kids who know they are needed, who play an active part in the real, day-to-day work of their family, do better in school because they feel a part of something more significant than themselves. Working hard and doing well in school are natural by-products of this commitment to their family group. Very important people are depending on them to do their best.

All kids are able to help out, and all kids profit from the experience. They'll feel a sense of accomplishment that is unique because it's earned.

How To Do It: Anyone can hand out duties like a first sergeant. And anyone can get the same results—grumbling, ill-tempered troops just going through the motions, not really doing a good job.

Learning Allies do four things that make daily chores productive and rewarding parts of family life for their youngsters:

1. **Make the chores fair.**

Learning Allies recognize that kids are ignorant of a lot of things, but they are experts when it comes to fairness. They have strong and immediate reactions to work assignments that are perceived to be arbitrary, difficult, or meaningless.

Prior to assigning work, take the time to consider just what you are asking your youngster to do. Decide if it is within their ability and then add just a pinch more to make it a challenge. Give them assignments that are on a par with the duties of other members in the household, including the adults. Finally, make sure the chore is worthy of their efforts and contributes to the common good.

2. Check the chores out with the kid.

Once you have some chores you feel are meaningful and fair, run them by your youngster. Getting their input is often the key to getting the job done. Adults often avoid this step because they're afraid of being wimps. They feel being authoritative and directive is the only thing that works. It's not.

None of us likes to be steamrolled with someone else's laundry list of demands. Kids are no different. They are more likely to invest themselves in work they have some role in defining. Be willing to negotiate, and recognize that you can build on small successes. Giving in a little on the amount of work you think is appropriate can often set the scene for rewarding experiences that motivate your kid to volunteer for more.

3. Let the kid *do* the work.

If the only way a job can be done is *your* way, do it yourself! Don't hand it out as a chore—you are just setting your youngster up for failure. The kid can't be you. They can only be themselves, and thus their approach to the work will be unique. Learning Allies know that tolerating this individual approach to chores is pivotal to making them meaningful, and even fun.

"We work to become, not to acquire."

Elbert Hubbard

Avoid the trap of trying to create clones of yourself by defining, with your youngster, the outcomes or final objectives of their work. Let them determine how the actual work will be done. You concern yourself with making it clear what the end result will look like, and when it should look that way. This demonstrates your respect for their skill and judgment. With the space you provide them, they may even ask for advice.

4. Deliver the payoff.

Some kids get paid an hourly wage for their duties. Others have the fees rolled into their allowance. A few get a hug and a "Job well done!" Regardless, every young person who successfully attends to their daily chores expects a payday. Learning Allies know this and agree in advance on the conditions of the contract. Then they never miss a payroll.

Kids deserve to know what is realistic and appropriate payment in their family. Overpayment can be as damaging as underpayment, so ask around, and see what makes sense in your "real world." In the end, pay them the greatest bonus of all by giving genuine praise and showing admiration for their good work.

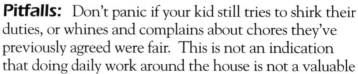

Pitfalls: Don't panic if your kid still tries to shirk their duties, or whines and complains about chores they've previously agreed were fair. This is not an indication that doing daily work around the house is not a valuable experience. It's just evidence that your kid is normal. Persevere, and don't get caught up in harsh judgments. Listen to their concerns and try to accommodate differences in work-style and timing. Focus on the end product and bend over backwards supporting them in its achievement. Remember that some kids just need to moan and groan while they work.

Afterword

Go Ahead, Give It A Try!

▲ ▲

OK, let's see how much of your time it will take to be a Learning Ally. Let me do a little work on my calculator. Yes, I think that's it. If you do everything I say a Learning Ally should do, you'll have ***exactly one hour and eleven minutes*** left in each day to earn a living, carry on a relationship, pursue your hobbies, and get some quality-time for yourself.

Hmmm, wait a minute, that doesn't sound right. Let me check those calculations. There must be something amiss here. The math is right . . . oh yeah, I remember! ***You're not supposed to do everything I say you should!***

Everything in this book is not appropriate for you and your youngster. Some of it is right on the mark and some just doesn't fit. As I said in the introduction, you have to wander around and make some judgments as to what will work. In the end, your genuine efforts as a Learning Ally will propel your kid's success. The strategies I've presented give you some good direction, but you must follow your own heading.

There are times when that personal heading takes you into uncharted waters. All your efforts as a Learning Ally and all the help of your child's teacher are not enough. Don't hesitate to get professional help when you hit an impasse. A Learning Ally also knows when to call in the reinforcements of educational specialists, counselors, and medical personnel. I do hope, though, that you'll consider some of the advice that seems a little far-fetched before you count yourself out of the game. For it's stretching yourself in this fashion that really builds your power as an ally in your youngster's learning.

When your initial reaction is, "Oh no, that's not me. I can't see myself succeeding at ***that,***" take a moment to consider your response. Are you really so sure you'll fail? Or are you more concerned about your own comfort level? Remember, a little discomfort is often the price of progress.

So if something I've suggested seems to have potential, go ahead and give it a try. Your genuine intent is the critical factor, not the perfection of your effort. Remember, kids are very forgiving and they'll always admire you for taking a risk.

The fact that you are reading this book means you're a person of action. You've chosen not to take the greatest gamble of all, and that is to do nothing. Positive, constructive activity on your part stimulates the same behavior in your kid. It's the only sure thing in this whole business of being a Learning Ally. Doing something always beats doing nothing.

If you haven't done so already, go back over the suggestions in this book and find one or two that seem to have potential for you and your youngster. Combine my ideas with your own good sense and take charge of your child's education by becoming a Learning Ally.

▲ ▲ ▲

Terry Mallen invites all Learning Allies to share their successes and challenges, which will support his ongoing research in this area. Please include as much biographical data as possible, i.e., ages, grade level of student, schooling, employment, and marital status of adult. Send to:

Terry Mallen
c/o ACUMEN Press
P. O. Box 16385
Seattle, WA 98116

Don't Borrow This Book When You Can Have a Copy of Your Own. Order One Now!

"Taking Charge of Your Child's Education" Makes a Great Gift, Too!

Call for quantity discounts on a dozen or more books for your company, group or class.

▲▲▲

Order Toll Free! Call 1-800-468-1994
Visa, Mastercard accepted

Order By Mail:
Send to: ACUMEN Press ▪ P.O. Box 16385 ▪ Seattle, WA 98116

Your SHIPPING information:
company_____

name_____

street address_____ Apt. or Suite#_____

city_____ state_____ zip_____

phone (_____)_____

Your BILLING information:
company_____

name_____

address_____ Apt. or Suite#_____

city_____ state_____ zip_____

phone (_____)_____

Payment: ☐ MC ☐ VISA ☐ Check

Make Checks Payable to: **Acumen Press**

Card No:_____

Exp. Date:_____ Issuing Bank:_____

Qty	Price each	TOTAL
	$14.95 U.S. ▪ $19.95 Canadian	
	Shipping ($3 each)	
WA Residents add 8.2% sales tax ($1.47 per book)		
	TOTAL	

Don't Borrow This Book When You Can Have a Copy of Your Own. Order One Now!

"Taking Charge of Your Child's Education" Makes a Great Gift, Too!

Call for quantity discounts on a dozen or more books for your company, group or class.

▲▲▲

Order Toll Free! Call 1-800-468-1994
Visa, Mastercard accepted

Order By Mail:
Send to: ACUMEN Press ▪ P.O. Box 16385 ▪ Seattle, WA 98116

Your SHIPPING information:
company_____

name _____

street address _____ Apt. or Suite# _____

city_____ state_____ zip _____

phone (_____)_____

Your BILLING information:
company_____

name_____

address_____ Apt. or Suite# _____

city_____ state _____ zip _____

phone (_____)_____

Payment: ☐ MC ☐ VISA ☐ Check
Make Checks Payable to: **Acumen Press**
Card No:_____
Exp. Date:_____ Issuing Bank: _____

Qty	Price each	TOTAL
	$14.95 U.S. ▪ $19.95 Canadian	
	Shipping ($3 each)	
WA Residents add 8.2% sales tax ($1.47 per book)		
	TOTAL	